BIBLICAL INTERPRETATION:
The Only Right Way

David Kuske

NORTHWESTERN PUBLISHING HOUSE
Milwaukee, Wisconsin

Library of Congress Card 95-69594
Northwestern Publishing House
1250 N. 113th St., Milwaukee, WI 53226-3284
© 1995 by Northwestern Publishing House.
Published 1995
Printed in the United States of America
ISBN 0-8100-0572-7

TABLE OF CONTENTS

PART TWO:
THE HISTORY OF INTERPRETATION FROM
THE TIME OF CHRIST

PART THREE:
THREE HISTORICAL-CRITICAL METHODS
OF INTERPRETATION

INTRODUCTION

People from different churches who discuss religion with one another soon discover a fact that repeats itself fairly often. A person from one church understands a passage of the Bible quite differently from the way a person from another church understands that very same passage. Why does this happen? Both have the same the Bible and maybe even the same translation of the Bible. Both may belong to Christian churches that claim to use the Bible as the basic source of doctrine. How can they conclude that a Bible verse means two different things?

In this time of religious toleration, many people answer that question by saying, "It's just a matter of interpretation." What that statement basically does is give credence to the idea that the words of the Bible can be interpreted in many different ways. What people really mean when they say this is, "It's just a matter of perspective." If you read the Bible from the perspective of your own church, you might well come up with one understanding of a Bible passage. A person from a church with a different perspective ends up with a different understanding.

It is the goal of this book to show that proper interpretation is never a subjective matter of different people's perspectives.

"It's just a matter of interpretation." That is a lie by which Satan leads many souls to eternal destruction. This lie asserts that the problem is really with the Bible. The Bible can be understood in many different ways, the devil whispers, so no one ought to insist that his understanding is the only right one. Above all, Satan argues, people should not separate from one another because they understand the Bible differently. They ought to work together patiently and lovingly so that maybe somewhere down the road they can work out a compromise, a common understanding of what the Bible says that all religions can accept.

"It's just a matter of interpretation." This lie of the devil implies that there are many different ways to go about interpreting the Bible. But that just isn't true! It is the major goal of this book to show that there is only one right way to interpret the Bible.

1

INTERPRETING THE BIBLE
IS UNIQUE IN ONLY ONE WAY

Interpretation is part of our everyday life

Interpretation is not something we do only when we read the Bible. We practice interpretation every time we listen to someone speak or whenever we read something in print. For example, when we see the five letters *a, e, r, t,* and *w* put together in a sequence to form the word *water,* we interpret that word (whether we are hearing or reading it) to be referring to the liquid that we drink or use for washing.

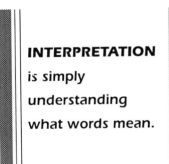

INTERPRETATION is simply understanding what words mean.

The letters of the alphabet and the sounds we attach to them are symbols by which we form words. We can put those 26 symbols into different sequences to form different words. Obviously, in order to communicate with one another, we need to be able to interpret what those words mean.

Some words, like *waterfall,* convey only one basic thought. Other words, like *water,* convey thoughts that are related, yet a bit different. As a noun, *water* refers to the liquid we drink to quench our thirst. As a verb, it refers to using water to sprinkle or soak something (e.g., I need to water the lawn.) Still other words convey two or more thoughts that are not related to one another. For example, *ram* can be a verb meaning to crash against something in a violent way. As a noun it may refer either to a male sheep or to the random-access memory of a computer.

How do we know which meaning to attach to words that can mean different things? The **context** helps us interpret because the context tells us how words are being used. Context tells us whether *ram* and *water* are being used as nouns or verbs, as well as which meaning of *ram* as a noun is meant.

The CONTEXT is the key factor in the right interpretation of what words mean.

The context will also determine different shadings of meaning that words or phrases can have. Note that in the following three sentences the meaning of the phrase *I'm glad* has three different shadings. In the first sentence, it expresses pleasure; in the second, relief; in the third, sarcasm.

I'm glad you were able to attend our reunion.

I'm glad I got over that cough.

I'm glad you know everything that happened even though you weren't there.

In these sentences, the interpretation of the different shadings of *I'm glad* is clear to us just by the context of the sentences themselves. Other examples could be given where it may be necessary to have several sentences of the context in order to properly interpret the meaning of a word or phrase within a given sentence.

It's also true that changing the location of words in a sentence can change the meaning of the whole sentence. Note how this happens when the location of one word, *only,* is changed in the following four sentences:

He thought he could turn only at the corner.

He thought he could only turn at the corner.

He thought only he could turn at the corner.

He only thought he could turn at the corner.

Distinguishing the different meanings of these sentences may require a second reading of them. But in the end, we can clearly interpret what each of them means.

These examples illustrate the fact that interpretation is not limited to the activity of reading the Bible. We use the basic principles of interpretation every day in communicating with one another. In reading the Bible we simply apply those same principles to written words as they are used in their biblical context.

The objective of Bible interpretation

In interpreting written symbols of any kind, the inter-preter's purpose must always be to *determine the meaning that the original writer intended for the original reader*—nothing more, nothing less. So, when the interpreter paraphrases what the original writer meant to say to the original reader, it must be  **SAYS** equals **MEANS** exactly what the writer said to that reader—nothing more, nothing less. A basic equation, SAYS = MEANS, will be used often in this book to underscore this point.

This equation is a basic rule that must govern all communication; otherwise, what people said or wrote to one another would obviously be confusing at best. The only exception to this basic rule might be the situation in which the sender and the receiver of a message agreed to communicate in code in order to hide the actual meaning of that message from others.

What is true for everyday interpretation is doubly true in Bible interpretation because we are interpreting what God says. In the process of determining what the Bible says and means, the interpreter must be careful not to inject anything *subjective* into his interpretation. If he does, he is replacing what God says and means with his own personal ideas. The

13

SAYS = MEANS interpretation equation is kept in proper balance only if the interpreter determines objectively what the biblical author meant based solely on what he said. Part One of this book (chapters 2–7) will present six principles that are basic to objective interpretation.

But in order for the contemporary interpreter of the Bible to know what the original writer meant to say to the original reader, he must bridge two sizable gaps: the language gap and the culture gap. What complicates the task even more is that the language and culture involved existed 2,000 years ago. If we remember that it took only about one generation for the word *square* (when used to describe a person) to change in meaning from "honest" to "out of touch," we get a little better idea of why the passing of time adds to the challenge of bridging the language and culture gaps.

The language gap can be bridged fairly well if one uses a reliable translation. "Reliable" in this instance means a translation that accurately reflects what the words and sentences meant to the original reader. But a translation can never fully bridge the language gap because some shades of meaning

LANGUAGE GAP

and some nuances of grammar in the Hebrew and Greek languages can never be captured fully in English.

For example, the Greek word translated *perseverance* in Romans 5:3 ("suffering produces perseverance") expresses the double idea of patience combined with perseverance. Since we have no equivalent word in English that combines these same two ideas, the English translation does not quite express everything the Greek word says and means. Or consider Jesus' words from the cross: "It is finished." Again the Greek says a little more than the English translation. Here a tense is used in Greek that expresses the idea that an action was completed that had continuing results. Thus the full meaning of what Jesus said is not only that his work of salvation was finished, but also that this action has results that are permanent.

These examples show that the interpreter who uses a reliable English translation will not end up with a wrong inter-

14

pretation. The meaning of the verse isn't changed. Instead, the interpreter just may not be able to acquire the full meaning of some verses from the translation. Using our equation, we could say something like this. In most verses the SAYS = MEANS equation will be maintained. In a few verses, however, what happens in interpretation might look more like this: SAYS = means. This fact also helps us understand why we want our pastors who serve as our spiritual shepherds to be able to work with the Bible in the original languages.

There also is a culture gap because things that were common in the various places and times in which the books of the Bible were written are not part of our lives today. Our wedding and funeral customs are different. The way we farm, our climate, our cities, our economic and political and social systems—all are different from those of biblical times.

CULTURE GAP

An example may help make the significance of the culture gap a little clearer. In Proverbs 19:12 we read that a king's favor "is like dew on the grass." Dew in many parts of the United States is not a welcome thing. It sometimes delays a busy farmer from getting an early start in baling hay, and the person who lives in town may not be too happy when he gets his shoes all wet walking across the lawn in the morning. But in Palestine, the dew was not only welcome, it was vital because it provided moisture each day for the growing crops during the long dry season. The person who doesn't know this and thinks of dew from the perspective of our country might have a difficult time trying to figure out what this passage in Proverbs means.

This example also illustrates that, while a person can understand what the words are saying, he may not know exactly what they mean. He shouldn't end up with a wrong meaning because he will understand from the context that this Proverbs passage means to say that the king's favor is something good. But just exactly why this simile was used may escape the interpreter who hasn't bridged the culture gap in this instance. For this verse his interpretation equation will be something like this: SAYS = means (?).

The culture gap is usually easier to bridge than the language gap. One doesn't have to learn Hebrew or Greek. Instead, the interpreter can read helpful books and articles on: the geography of Palestine, the Mediterranean area, and the East; the plants and animals of Palestine; the food and clothing of biblical times; the kind of homes people lived in and how they conducted their daily lives; and so on.

The principles that the interpreter uses in bridging the language gap and the culture gap are obviously two of the subjects that a study of biblical interpretation must address. This is done at some length in two later chapters (6 and 7), which deal with the historical and grammatical settings of Scripture.

The spiritual gap— the unique aspect of Bible interpretation

Before leaving the subject of gaps that must be bridged, it is imperative that we also take note of a third gap, the spiritual gap. As was noted earlier, if the language and culture gaps are not bridged, the Bible interpreter has a definite handicap. But usually the worst that will happen is that the MEANS part of the interpretation equation may be left somewhat incomplete in given verses. But failing to bridge the spiritual gap will inevitably have more serious consequences. It will cause the interpreter to change or even destroy the basic equation of SAYS = MEANS.

SPIRITUAL

GAP

The attitude that is basic to proper Bible interpretation is a result of the Holy Spirit working saving faith in a person's heart. God makes it clear that such a faith is indispensable for a Bible interpreter when he says in 1 Corinthians 2:14: "The *man without the Spirit* does not accept the things that come from the Spirit of God, for they are *foolishness* to him, and he *cannot understand* them, because they are spiritually discerned." Obviously, a person who considers what he is reading to be foolishness will not do a good job of interpreting; and if he can't understand what is said, his interpretation is not going to be the right one.

Scripture also states that no one is neutral where God and his Word are concerned. Before the Spirit brings a person to faith in Christ, that person is by nature completely opposed to everything that comes from God. Romans 8:5-7 says, "Those who live according to the sinful nature have their *minds set on what that nature desires;* but those who live in accordance with the Spirit have their minds set on what the Spirit desires. The mind of sinful man is death, but the mind controlled by the Spirit is life and peace; *the sinful mind is hostile to God.*" Jesus put the impossibility of neutrality in spiritual matters very simply when he said, "He who is not with me is against me" (Matthew 12:30).

The fact that no one is spiritually neutral has obvious consequences for biblical interpretation. It is impossible for anyone to read Scripture without presuppositions. Either, one reads it with an unbelieving mind and his interpretation reflects this (usually by denying that the Bible really MEANS what it SAYS) or, one reads the Bible with a believing mind, following the Spirit in faith (simply letting SAYS = MEANS). There is no in-between; there is no neutral mind when it comes to interpreting Scripture.

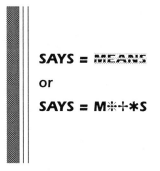

SAYS = MEANS

or

SAYS = M*+*S

It is possible for an unbeliever to know in an outward way what the words of Scripture are saying. But it is not possible for him to know them in the same way that the believer does. The unbeliever will not read Scripture with a childlike and confident trust that these words mean exactly what they say and that they are the truth. Because the unbeliever either cannot understand or cannot accept the spiritual meaning of the words of Scripture, he will either deny their meaning or change the meaning to something he can accept. In either case, he sets aside the equation that is basic to all communication (SAYS = MEANS). Then he also has to make up an excuse why he can do this with the Bible even though he knows he can't do this with any other written book or document.

Presuppositions of faith

The assertion that God's Word can be read without any presuppositions is, as we have just seen, something that God, the author of Scripture, says is impossible. It is also an assertion which is often made to undermine these two truths that God declares about the Bible:

1. All Scripture centers in Christ (Christocentric).
2. All Scripture was written by men under the guidance of the Holy Spirit so that all the words of the Bible are God's Word (verbally inspired and inerrant).

These two truths are the two presuppositions that are basic to proper biblical interpretation. We call these two truths "presuppositions of faith" because the faith that the Holy Spirit works in us also convinces us that these presuppositions are true. The Holy Spirit not only leads us to accept Christ as our Savior. He also creates in us the certainty that everything Jesus tells us is the truth. By faith we know, as John 14:6 says, that Jesus is not only the Way and the Life, he is also the Truth.

Jesus says in John 7:17 and 8:47 that everyone who believes ("chooses to do God's will," "belongs to God") will listen to what he says ("hears what God says") because they know that his "teaching comes from God." Therefore, when our Savior tells us that the Bible centers in him and·that it is verbally inspired, we know by faith that these are facts that can be trusted.

All Scripture centers in Christ

Jesus stated clearly that the Old Testament centers in him:

John 5:39 You diligently study the Scriptures because you think that by them you possess eternal life. These are the *Scriptures* that *testify about me.*

Luke 24:27 And beginning with *Moses and all the Prophets,* he explained to them what was said *in all the Scriptures concerning himself.*

Jesus also told the apostles who wrote the New Testament that what the Holy Spirit would guide them to write would bring glory to him:

John 16:14 He will *bring glory to me* by taking from what is mine and making it known to you.

Peter in his sermons and epistles stressed that the whole Old Testament pointed to Christ:

Acts 3:18 But this is how God fulfilled what he had foretold *through all the prophets,* saying that his Christ would suffer.

Acts 3:24 Indeed, *all the prophets* from Samuel on, as many as have spoken, have foretold these days.

Acts 10:42,43 He commanded us to preach to the people and to testify that he is the one whom God appointed as judge of the living and the dead. *All the prophets* testify about him that everyone who believes in him receives forgiveness of sins through his name."

1 Peter 1:10-12 Concerning this salvation, *the prophets,* who spoke of the grace that was to come to you, searched intently and with the greatest care, trying to find out the time and circumstances to which the Spirit of Christ in them was pointing when he predicted the sufferings of Christ and the glories that would follow. It was revealed to them that they were not serving themselves but you, when *they spoke of the things* that have now been told you by those who have preached the gospel to you by the Holy Spirit sent from heaven. Even angels long to look into these things.

Peter also emphasized that the New Testament apostles had one goal. They wanted to focus the believers' hearts on a true and thorough knowledge of Christ:

2 Peter 1:16 We did not follow cleverly invented stories when *we told you about the power and coming of our Lord Jesus Christ,* but we were eyewitnesses of his majesty.

2 Peter 3:2 I want you to recall the words spoken in the past by the holy prophets and the command given *by our Lord and Savior through your apostles.*

In all his epistles, Paul, too, centers his message in Christ:

> 1 Corinthians 2:2 For I resolved to *know nothing* while I was with you *except Jesus Christ* and him crucified.

> Ephesians 2:20 built on the foundation of the apostles and prophets, with *Christ Jesus himself as the chief cornerstone.*

> 2 Timothy 3:15 and how from infancy you have known the holy Scriptures, which are able to *make you wise for salvation* through faith *in Christ Jesus.*

All Scripture is verbally inspired

In a miraculous way, which goes beyond any human investigation, the Holy Spirit inspired chosen men to write God's Word. Each of the following passages states that the Bible writers spoke only as God directed or guided them:

> 2 Peter 1:21 For prophecy never had its origin in the will of man, but men *spoke from God as they were carried along by the Holy Spirit.*

> Hebrews 1:1 In the past *God spoke* to our forefathers *through the prophets* at many times and in various ways.

> Matthew 1:22 All this took place to fulfill what the *Lord had said through the prophet.*

> John 14:26 But the Counselor, *the Holy Spirit,* whom the Father will send in my name, *will teach you all things* and *will remind you of everything I have said to you.*

> John 16:13,14 But when he, the Spirit of truth, comes, he *will guide you* into all truth. He will not speak on his own; he will speak only what he hears, and *he will tell you* what is yet to come. He will bring glory to me by taking from what is mine and *making it known to you.*

The inspired writers wrote under varying circumstances:

1. What they wrote came from personal experience.

> 2 Peter 1:16 We did not follow cleverly invented stories when we told you about the power and coming of our Lord Jesus Christ, but *we were eyewitnesses* of his majesty.

2. What they wrote came from hearing what others said or from reading what others wrote.

> Luke 1:1-4 *Many have undertaken to draw up an account of the things that have been fulfilled among us,* just as they were handed down to us by those who from the first were eyewitnesses and servants of the word. Therefore, since *I myself have carefully investigated everything* from the beginning, it seemed good also to me to write an orderly account for you, most excellent Theophilus, so that you may know the certainty of the things you have been taught.

3. What they wrote came directly from God as a special kind of revelation.

> Acts 4:25 *You spoke by the Holy Spirit through the mouth of your servant,* our father David: "Why do the nations rage and the peoples plot in vain?"

> 1 Corinthians 2:13 This is *what we speak,* not in words taught us by human wisdom but in *words taught by the Spirit,* expressing spiritual truths in spiritual words.

> Revelation 1:10,11 I heard behind me a loud voice like a trumpet, which said: *"Write on a scroll what you see* and send it to the seven churches: to Ephesus, Smyrna, Pergamum, Thyatira, Sardis, Philadelphia and Laodicea."

Each writer used his own style and vocabulary. Yet every thought they expressed and every word they used was given them by inspiration of the Holy Spirit. Note in the last passage listed below that inspiration also included censoring. John intended to write something, but he was told not to do so.

> 1 Corinthians 2:13 This is what we speak, not in words taught us by human wisdom but in *words taught by the Spirit,* expressing spiritual truths in spiritual words.

> 2 Timothy 3:16 *All Scripture is God-breathed* and is useful for teaching, rebuking, correcting and training in righteousness.

> John 10:35 If he called them "gods," *to whom the word of God came*—and the *Scripture cannot be broken* . . .

Matthew 5:18 I tell you the truth, until heaven and earth disappear, not the smallest letter, *not the least stroke of a pen, will by any means disappear* from the Law until everything is accomplished.

John 17:17 Sanctify them by the truth; *your word is truth.*

Revelation 10:4 And when the seven thunders spoke, *I was about to write;* but I heard a voice from heaven say, "Seal up what the seven thunders have said and *do not write it down."*

Sometimes people argue that there are three things which cast doubt on the verbal inspiration of Scripture: variant readings, differing accounts of the same events, and different doctrinal emphases. These arguments will be examined later in chapters 5 and 8. There it will be shown that none of them cast any doubt on inspiration. They are merely arguments contrived by some to undermine or to reject the presuppositions of faith.

Four facets of biblical interpretation

In reading any portion of Scripture, the interpreter needs to remember four things about the Bible at all times: (1) It is an *ancient text* that was copied by hand for many centuries; (2) It is a *historical document;* (3) It is a *literary work;* and (4) It is a *sacred Scripture.*

The Bible is an *ancient text* which God chose to preserve for many centuries by hand copying rather than by preserving the original writings. This hand copying led to variant readings coming into the biblical text. Therefore, the interpreter will first have to consider variant readings in working with some verses of Scripture.

The Bible is also a *historical document* in which God chose to reveal his saving truth within the framework of many historical, geographical, and cultural contexts. Therefore, the interpreter will often have to consider the historical setting in working with large portions of Scripture.

The Bible is also a *literary document* in which God communicates with us in human language. Therefore, the interpreter must be governed in what he says the Bible means by the rules of syntax as determined by usage in the biblical languages (Hebrew, Aramaic, Greek). This is the grammatical setting of Scripture.

In all three of the previous considerations, the Bible is like any other book, and it must be read as one would read any other written document. However, the Bible is also a *sacred Scripture*. This means that this book must be read with the spiritual presuppositions laid down by its divine author. Because of his unregenerate heart and mind, the unbeliever rejects these presuppositions as foolishness. Since saving faith worked by the Holy Spirit is an absolute requisite for understanding both what Scripture says and means, only the believer will interpret the Bible without violating the basic equation of SAYS = MEANS. This is the one unique facet of Bible interpretation.

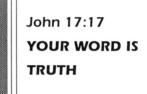

John 17:17

YOUR WORD IS TRUTH

BIBLIOGRAPHY—CHAPTER ONE

Lawrenz, C. J. (ed.). *This Steadfast Word.* Lutheran Free Conference Publications, 1965. pp. 4-42.

Mickelsen, A. B. *Interpreting the Bible.* Grand Rapids: William B. Eerdmans Publishing Co., 1963. pp. 54-95.

Surburg, R. F. *The Principles of Biblical Interpretation.* Fort Wayne: Concordia Theological Seminary Press, 1986. pp. 1-67.

Zuck, R. B. *Basic Bible Interpretation.* Wheaton, IL: Scripture Press-Victor Books, 1991. pp. 76-142.

Part One

SIX PRINCIPLES
OF
BIBLICAL INTERPRETATION

INTRODUCTION TO PART ONE

Chapter 2 begins the first and most important part of this treatment of Bible interpretation. In this part the emphasis will be on the principles that are basic to the proper interpretation of Scripture.

Each of the six chapter titles in Part One is a statement of one of the basic principles of interpretation. The word "only" in each principle underscores how sound interpretation differs from any false method of interpretation.

The first two principles (chapters 2 and 3) deal with two views of the Bible by which the enemies of God's Word try to undermine and deny what Scripture says.

Chapter 4 presents a short summary of how the interpreter handles variants in the New Testament text. A more in-depth treatment of this subject is presented in *The History and Practice of New Testament Textual Criticism* (Mequon, WI: Wisconsin Lutheran Seminary Press, 1994).

The last three chapters are the heart of Part One. They deal with the three key elements the interpreter must consider in explaining what any part of Scripture says and means. These key elements are: the historical setting, the grammatical setting, and the scriptural setting (i.e., the use of Scripture to interpret Scripture).

2

THE ONLY BOOKS
THAT ARE GOD'S WORD
ARE THE CANONICAL BOOKS
OF THE BIBLE

The authority of the canonical books

We recognize 39 Old Testament and 27 New Testament books as canonical. The term *canonical* reflects the basic meaning of the Greek word *kanon*. Originally this word referred to a measuring stick. Eventually it also came to mean a "rule" or a "standard" by which things were judged. When we speak of the 66 books as canonical, we are referring to them as the authoritative Word of God. We believe that these 66 books are the ones by which everything must be judged in our faith and life, our doctrine and practice. Only those books which are verbally inspired have this kind of authority.

The inner testimony of these books

How do we know whether a book is inspired or not? An inspired book has words that are "living and active."

Hebrews 4:12 For the word of God is *living and active.*
Sharper than any double-edged sword, it penetrates

> even to dividing soul and spirit, joints and marrow; it judges the thoughts and attitudes of the heart.

Because of this, these words impress themselves deeply on our hearts when we hear or read them.

> Hebrews 4:12 For the word of God is living and active. Sharper than any double-edged sword, it *penetrates* even to dividing soul and spirit, joints and marrow; it *judges* the thoughts and attitudes of the heart.

> Luke 24:32 They asked each other, "Were not our *hearts burning* within us while he talked with us on the road and *opened the Scriptures to us?*"

In this way an inspired book is self-authenticating. It creates a living faith in us (John 6:63) and brings about a faith-worked conviction that what we are hearing or reading is the truth (John 17:17).

> John 6:63 The Spirit gives life; the flesh counts for nothing. The *words* I have spoken to you are spirit and they *are life.*

> John 17:17 *Sanctify them* by the truth; your word is truth.

One of the ways, then, that we know these canonical books are inspired is their convincing inner testimony in our hearts.

The establishing of the Old Testament canon

In addition to this inner testimony, we have the testimony of Jesus and the New Testament apostles. At Jesus' time the Old Testament canon consisted of 39 books and had three major divisions: the law of Moses, the prophets, and the psalms.

JESUS authenticated the 39 books of the OT canon.

> Luke 24:44 He said to them, "This is what I told you while I was still with you: Everything must be fulfilled that is written about me in *the Law of Moses, the Prophets and the Psalms.*"

Jesus regularly spoke of these books as God's Word, and he said that they cannot be broken.

> John 10:35 If he called them "gods," to whom the word of God came—and *the Scripture cannot be broken* . . .

Paul and Peter also spoke of these Old Testament Scriptures as the inspired Word of God.

> 2 Timothy 3:16 *All Scripture is God-breathed* and is useful for teaching, rebuking, correcting and training in righteousness.

> 2 Peter 1:19-21 And we have *the word of the prophets* made more certain, and you will do well to pay attention to it, as to a light shining in a dark place, until the day dawns and the morning star rises in your hearts. Above all, you must understand that no prophecy of Scripture came about by the prophet's own interpretation. For prophecy never had its origin in the will of man, but *men spoke from God as they were carried along by the Holy Spirit.*

The establishing of the New Testament canon

Jesus withdrew his visible presence from the earth before the New Testament books were written. How, then, was the New Testament canon established? This was done by Jesus' chosen apostles.

One of the purposes for which Jesus chose his apostles was that they might speak in his name after his ascension. He also promised to send the Holy Spirit to them in a special way to guide them in this work.

> John 14:16,17 And I will ask the Father, and he will give you another *Counselor to be with you forever*—the Spirit of truth. The world cannot accept him, because it neither sees him nor knows him. But you know him, for he lives with you and will be in you.

> John 14:26 But the Counselor, the Holy Spirit, whom the Father will send in my name, will *teach you all things* and will *remind you of everything I have said to you.*

> John 16:5-7 Now I am going to him who sent me, yet none of you asks me, "Where are you going?" Because I have said these things, you are filled with grief. But I tell you the truth: It is *for your good that I am going away.*

> Unless I go away, the Counselor will not come to you; but if I go, I will send him to you.

> John 16:12-15 I have *much more to say to you,* more than you can now bear. But when he, the *Spirit of truth,* comes, he *will guide you into all truth.* He will not speak on his own; he will speak only what he hears, and he will tell you what is yet to come. He will bring glory to me by taking from what is mine and *making it known to you.* All that belongs to the Father is mine. That is why I said the Spirit will take from what is mine and make it known to you.

The apostles often reminded believers that their words were the Spirit's words.

> 1 Corinthians 2:12,13 *We have* not *received* the spirit of the world but *the Spirit who is from God,* that we may understand what God has freely given us. *This is what we speak,* not in words taught us by human wisdom but *in words taught by the Spirit,* expressing spiritual truths in spiritual words.

> 2 Peter 1:12-21 So *I will always remind you of these things,* even though you know them and are firmly established in the truth you now have. I think it is right to refresh your memory as long as I live in the tent of this body, because I know that I will soon put it aside, as our Lord Jesus Christ has made clear to me. And I will make every effort to see that after my departure you will always be able to remember these things. *We did not follow cleverly invented stories* when we told you about the power and coming of our Lord Jesus Christ, but we were eyewitnesses of his majesty. For he received honor and glory from God the Father when the voice came to him from the Majestic Glory, saying, "This is my Son, whom I love; with him I am well pleased." We ourselves heard this voice that came from heaven when we were with him on the sacred mountain. And *we have the word of the prophets* made more certain, and you will do well to pay attention to it, as to a light shining in a dark place, until the day dawns and the morning star rises in your hearts. Above all, you must understand that *no prophecy of Scripture came about by the prophet's own*

interpretation. For prophecy never had its origin in the will of man, but men spoke from God as they were carried along by the Holy Spirit.

The apostles indicated that the words they spoke were, therefore, on a par with the Old Testament Scriptures.

2 Peter 3:2 I want you to recall the words spoken in the past *by the holy prophets* and the command given by our Lord and Savior *through your apostles.*

Ephesians 2:20 . . . built on *the foundation of the apostles and prophets,* with Christ Jesus himself as the chief cornerstone.

The people who read these words received them as God's Word and shared these inspired writings with other congregations as the apostles urged them to do.

1 Thessalonians 2:13 And we also thank God continually because, when you received the word of God, which you heard from us, you accepted it not as the word of men, but *as it actually is, the word of God,* which is at work in you who believe.

Colossians 4:16 After this letter has been read to you, *see that it is also read in the church of the Laodiceans* and that you in turn read the letter from Laodicea.

1 Thessalonians 5:27 I charge you before the Lord to *have this letter read to all the brothers.*

Thus, collections of the New Testament books came into being with the encouragement and approval of the apostles.

2 Peter 3:15,16 Bear in mind that our Lord's patience means salvation, just as our dear brother *Paul also wrote you with the wisdom that God gave him.* He writes the same way *in all his letters,* speaking in them of these matters. His letters contain some things that are hard to understand, which ignorant and unstable people distort, as they do *the other Scriptures,* to their own destruction. (Note: Recall that according to 1 Peter 1:1, Peter writes these words to the Christians who were scattered in the many congregations all over Asia Minor.)

The apostles urged the believers to treasure God's Word, which included the books written by them, and to test everything by it.

> 1 Thessalonians 5:19-22 Do not put out the Spirit's fire; do not treat *prophecies* with contempt. *Test everything.* Hold on to the good. Avoid every kind of evil.

The apostles also warned Christians not to be misled by letters that falsely claimed to be apostolic.

> 2 Thessalonians 2:2 . . . not to become easily unsettled or alarmed by some *prophecy, report or letter supposed to have come from us,* saying that the day of the Lord has already come.

The apostle John was the author of the last book of the New Testament canon to be written. Late in the first century, the Lord Jesus (through John) commended the congregation in Ephesus for rejecting those false teachers who claimed that what they said was to be given equal status with the words of the apostles.

> Revelation 2:2 I know your deeds, your hard work and your perseverance. I know that you cannot tolerate wicked men, that *you have tested those who claim to be apostles* but are not, and have *found them false.*

JESUS' APOSTLES guided the collection and preservation of the books of the NT canon.

It is clear, then, that the apostles, to whom Jesus had given the Holy Spirit in a special measure for this very purpose, guided the collection and preservation of the inspired books of the New Testament. By inspiration, they wrote most of the New Testament books themselves. They gave apostolic approval to the other books, which were written under inspiration by their coworkers: Mark, Luke, James, Jude, and Hebrews (if the latter was not written by Paul).

The discussion of the New Testament canon that took place in the post-apostolic period did not establish the canon.

Rather, it was a discussion in which faithful leaders of the church defended the canon against the attacks of heretics and defined more clearly why these 27 books comprised the canon.

The antilegomena

At various times in the history of the church, questions have been raised about the canon. The books that have been widely accepted and never seriously challenged as part of the canon are called *homolegoumena*. The books that have been widely rejected and never seriously considered to be a part of the canon are called the *pseudepigrapha*. Books that have been added to the canon by some, notably the Roman Catholic Church, are called the *apocrypha*. And books that some have wanted to subtract from the canon are called the *antilegomena*.

The latter are worthy of further comment. In the Old Testament the books that some have wanted to remove include Esther, Proverbs, Song of Songs, Ecclesiastes, and Ezekiel. In the New Testament they include Hebrews, James, Peter, 2 John, 3 John, Jude, and Revelation. The arguments brought against the inclusion of these books in the canon usually involve either the content of the book or its authorship. For example, Luther expressed some doubts about James and Revelation because of their content.

When one considers the doubts or objections that have been expressed about the antilegomena, it becomes clear that the problem lies either with the person's lack of understanding or lack of information. The problem does not lie with the inspired book.

The post-Reformation Lutheran theologians (Chemnitz, Gerhard, Calov, Quenstedt) accepted the antilegomena as canonical, but they cautioned that these books should not be used to establish articles of faith. They urged that no doctrine be drawn from these books without clear support from the other canonical books. In essence this merely applied the principle that Scripture must interpret Scripture (see chapter 8) in a somewhat more restrictive way to these books.

The New Testament apocrypha
and the writings of the church fathers

Since the New Testament apocrypha and the many writings of the church fathers came into existence within the Christian church, some people assume that they are equal to the New Testament canonical books. In chapter 11, for example, we will see that some who follow the historical-critical method of interpretation are inclined to think that the gospel of Thomas has a more accurate account of one of Jesus' parables than Luke's gospel does.[1]

The apocrypha and the writings of the church fathers were penned by Christians. Therefore, they may be interesting and even important to note because they show us how Scripture was understood by some Christians in the early church. These writings may also be helpful in establishing the meaning of Greek words and syntactical usage. They may help us better understand some items involving the historical setting. But the men who wrote these books were not inspired by the Holy Spirit, so no one may use anything from these writings to alter or deny something contained in the canonical books.

> **Non-biblical literature may not be used to alter or deny any biblical statement.**

Non-Christian writings

Another way some people have tried to alter or deny the meaning of New Testament passages is by explaining a New Testament passage in the light of statements from non-Christian writings. This is usually done with quotes from these writings that are similar in some way to a passage in the Bible. Most of the time this is illegitimate interpretation because the person is viewing the words of Scripture through the eyes of a pagan writer.

For example, the liberal German theologian, Rudoph Bultmann (d. 1976), in his explanation of the Good Shepherd chapter (John 10), argues at length that the reciprocal relationship of the sheep and the shepherd (i.e., the shepherd calls and the sheep hear his voice) is not original. He says it is taken from the Mandaean literature of the Gnostic tradition.[2] From this viewpoint he concludes that the real meaning of the passage is that the shepherd is Jesus in his role as the existentialistic revealer of man's true existence. Chapter 10 gives a fuller explanation of what is meant by this.

Others use the writings of early Gnostics, the Essenes, the Eastern mystics, the Stoic and Epicurean philosophers, or the Jewish rabbis to alter or deny the real meaning of a passage. They do this, of course, because these interpreters do not accept the Bible as God's inspired and authoritative Word.

Instead, they consider the New Testament to be a book written by men who were greatly influenced in their writing by the pagan world in which they lived. Or, they view the Bible as the product of a Christian community that inevitably wove the thoughts of the people living around them into their sacred writings.

To change God's holy Word by explaining it in terms of human philosophy, pagan thought, or anti-Christian religions is blasphemy.

At the same time, we must be careful not to say that these religious writings of the New Testament time are of no value to us at all. If they are written in Greek, these writings can be helpful in giving us insights into meanings of individual Greek words or they may help us understand Greek syntax better. In this way they are as helpful as any other Greek literature of the time.

In addition, if these early writings touch on something that was part of the culture of those days (e.g., slavery), they may throw some light on the historical setting. But neither the secular nor the extra-canonical religious writings of New Testament times may be used to alter or deny any statement of Scripture in any way.

New "revelations"

Many sects of our day have been founded on so-called revelations from God. For example, a "revelation" that Joseph Smith supposedly received from God is proclaimed by the Mormons as a vital addition to the Old and New Testaments.

They use the Book of Mormon to supplement and explain the Bible. In the process, they change and deny some of the key teachings of Scripture, especially the way of salvation. Our Lord tells us to test every such "revelation" by the touchstone of his Word. When we do so and find that the "revelation" is man's word, we know that it is something that may not be used to alter or deny anything that Scripture says.

Summary

One of the attempts Satan uses to lead people astray in Bible interpretation is to cause confusion about the relationship of canonical and non-canonical writings. As a result, many people in our day want to interpret some or all of Scripture on the basis of many different kinds of non-canonical writings. Such interpretation is improper because no word of man can be used to change God's Word in any way or to deny any part of it. The only books which are God's Word are the canonical books of the Bible.

NOTES

[1]Rudolph Bultmann, *The Gospel of St. John* (Philadelphia: Westminster Press, 1971), pp. 367,374.

[2]*Concordia Theological Monthly,* 1972, pp. 558,559.

BIBLIOGRAPHY—CHAPTER TWO

Gawrisch, W. "How the Canonicity of the Bible Was Established." *Wisconsin Lutheran Quarterly,* Vol. 70, No. 2. pp. 94-119.

Geisler, N. L., and W. E. Nix. *From God to Us.* Chicago: Moody Press, 1981. pp. 62-125.

Wicke, H. "The Scriptures—The Canon." *Northwestern Lutheran,* March 15, 1981. pp. 88-90.

3

THE ONLY WORLDVIEW OF SCRIPTURE
IS THE SUPERNATURAL

The modern denial of the supernatural

For most Christians, the principle stated in the title of this chapter is an obvious one. This is what Scripture teaches. This is what anyone who was a Christian prior to the 1800s believed. As Christians we normally would assume that anyone who reads the Bible with faith reads this book with the understanding that there is a God. This God is not a mere observer of the human world. Rather, he created it and, after its fall into sin, he rescued it by sending his only Son as its Savior.

But this assumption is no longer true in our day. Satan has been quite successful in changing this basic worldview even among a large number of those who call themselves Christian. As a result, much of the Bible interpretation done in our day includes a denial of the supernatural in the Bible, either entirely or in part. We are referring to the method of interpretation known as the historical-critical method.

The historical-critical method of interpretation is unfortunately the most commonly accepted form of Bible interpretation in Christendom today. The historical-critical method has several varieties. Part Three of this book (chapters 10–13) will detail how several forms of this method differ from one another. But all the forms either deny or limit the supernatural worldview as it is presented in Scripture.

Verbal inspiration is denied or limited. Miracles are denied by some, explained away by others, and called unimportant by still others. The historical accounts of God's direction of events in history to carry out his saving plan is denied, questioned, or simply set aside as unimportant.

How do people arrive at these conclusions about the supernatural in Scripture? They insist that the words of Scripture must be subjected to "scientific" investigation. Form, source, and redaction criticism, which came directly out of rationalism's denial of the supernatural, are used to determine whether given passages in the Bible are actual historical accounts or not. As chapter 9 will show, this is rationalism's way of trying to set aside the supernatural and so also prove that Scripture is man's word rather than God's verbally inspired Word.

It is only because of the denial of the supernatural in our day that the principle of interpretation in this chapter needs to be stated. Any denial of the supernatural contradicts the basic scriptural worldview.

The scriptural worldview

Scripture presents the sad story of sinful mankind in which there is only one constant, namely, God in his grace and power working out his saving plan for all people. Ephesians 1:22 says that God has put all things under Jesus' control, that he might guide everything in the world in the interest of his believers.

> Ephesians 1:22 And God placed all things under his feet and appointed him to be head over everything *for the church.*

Psalm 2 summarizes the worldview of Scripture this way: The rulers of the world in their foolishness try to oppose the almighty God and his Son, the Savior. God laughs at them. He sends his Son to save the nations and to rule over everything. This brings consternation to those who oppose him and blessing to those who trust in him.

Psalm 2 Why do the nations conspire and the peoples plot in vain? The kings of the earth take their stand and *the rulers gather together against the* LORD *and against his Anointed One.* "Let us break their chains," they say, "and throw off their fetters." The One enthroned in heaven laughs; the Lord scoffs at them. Then he rebukes them in his anger and terrifies them in his wrath, saying, "*I have installed my King on Zion,* my holy hill." I will proclaim the decree of the LORD: He said to me, "You are my Son; today I have become your Father. Ask of me, and *I will make the nations your inheritance,* the ends of the earth your possession. You will rule them with an iron scepter; you will *dash them to pieces like pottery.*" Therefore, you kings, be wise; be warned, you rulers of the earth. Serve the LORD with fear and rejoice with trembling. Kiss the Son, lest he be angry and you be destroyed in your way, for his wrath can flare up in a moment. *Blessed are all who take refuge in him.*

Psalms 33 and 46 express over and over again the confidence of the believer. He knows that God is a God who not only watches over everything but also intervenes in the affairs of the world whenever he sees fit to do so according to his saving plan.

GOD directed and still directs historical events to accomplish his saving plan.

Psalm 33:10-22 *The* LORD *foils the plans of the nations; he thwarts the purposes of the peoples. But the plans of the* LORD *stand firm forever,* the purposes of his heart through all generations. Blessed is the nation whose God is the LORD, the people he chose for his inheritance. From heaven *the* LORD *looks down and sees all mankind;* from his dwelling place *he watches all who live on earth*—he who forms the hearts of all, who *considers everything they do.* No king is saved by the size of his army; no warrior escapes by his great strength. A horse is a vain hope for deliverance; despite all its great strength it cannot save. *But the eyes of the* LORD *are on those who fear him,* on those whose hope is in his unfailing love, to deliver them from death and keep them alive in famine. We wait in hope for the LORD; *he is our help and our shield.* In him our hearts rejoice, for we trust in his holy name. May your unfailing love rest upon us, O LORD, even as we put our hope in you.

Psalm 46 *God is our refuge and strength,* an *ever-present help in trouble.* Therefore we will not fear, though the earth give way and the mountains fall into the heart of the sea, though its waters roar and foam and the mountains quake with their surging. There is a river whose streams make glad the city of God, the holy place where the Most High dwells. God is within her, she will not fall; *God will help her at break of day.* Nations are in uproar, kingdoms fall; *he lifts his voice, the earth melts. The LORD Almighty is with us;* the God of Jacob is our fortress. *Come and see the works of the LORD,* the *desolations he has brought* on the earth. He *makes wars cease* to the ends of the earth; he *breaks the bow* and *shatters the spear,* he *burns the shields with fire.* "Be still, and know that *I am God; I will be exalted among the nations,* I will be exalted in the earth." *The LORD Almighty is with us;* the God of Jacob is our fortress.

In Acts 13:17-41 the inspired writer emphasizes that God intervened over and over again in the events of the world. The events that took place were not mere happenstance. Rather, everything was directed by him.

Acts 13:17-41 The *God* of the people of Israel *chose our fathers; he made the people prosper* during their stay in Egypt, with mighty power *he led them out* of that country, *he endured* their conduct for about forty years in the desert, *he overthrew* seven nations in Canaan and *gave their land* to his people as their inheritance. All this took about 450 years. After this, *God gave them judges* until the time of Samuel the prophet. Then the people asked for a king, and *he gave them Saul* son of Kish, of the tribe of Benjamin, who ruled forty years. *After removing Saul, he made David their king. He testified* concerning him: "I have found David son of Jesse a man after my own heart; he will do everything I want him to do." From this man's descendants *God has brought to Israel the Savior Jesus, as he promised* . . . Brothers, children of Abraham, and you God-fearing Gentiles, it is to us that this message of salvation has been sent. The people of Jerusalem and their rulers did not recognize Jesus, yet in condemning him they fulfilled the words of the prophets that are read every Sabbath. Though they found no proper ground for a death sentence, they asked Pilate to have him executed. When they had carried out all that was written about him, they took him down from the tree and laid him in a tomb. But *God raised him* from the dead . . . We tell you the good news: *What God promised our fathers he has fulfilled* for us, their children, by raising up Jesus . . . The one whom God raised from the dead did not see decay. Therefore, my brothers, I want you to know that through Jesus the forgiveness of sins is proclaimed to you. Through him everyone who believes is justified from everything you could not be justified from by the law of Moses. Take care that what the prophets have said does not happen to you: "Look, you scoffers, wonder and perish, *for I am going to do something* in your days that you would never believe, even if someone told you."

In these and numerous other passages like them, the Bible clearly teaches that God has directed history in the past and still does so today in order to accomplish his saving purpose.

Miracles

Scripture treats miracles as real events, not as figments of the imagination of people with nonscientific minds. Jesus cited his miracles as proof that he is both the Son of God and the promised Messiah.

> Jesus' **MIRACLES** proved that he is the Son of God and our Savior.

John 10:38 But if I do it, even though you do not believe me, *believe the miracles,* that you may *know and understand that the Father is in me, and I in the Father.*

John 14:11 *Believe me when I say that I am in the Father* and the Father is in me; or at least *believe on the evidence of the miracles* themselves.

Jesus and Peter pointed to the fact of the miracles Jesus did as a basis for God's judgment on those who denied him and crucified him.

> John 15:24 *If I had not done* among them what no one else did, *they would not be guilty of sin.* But now *they have seen these miracles,* and yet they have hated both me and my Father.

> Acts 2:22,23 Men of Israel, listen to this: Jesus of Nazareth was *a man accredited by God to you by miracles, wonders and signs, which God did among you through him,* as you yourselves know . . . You, with the help of wicked men, *put him to death* by nailing him to the cross.

The miracles of Jesus' virgin birth, his being both God and man in one person, his resurrection, and his ascension are keystones of God's plan of salvation. Without these miracles we have no Savior and no salvation.

MIRACLES are an essential part of Jesus' saving work. If these miracles are not true, our salvation never took place.

When the angel came to Joseph in a dream and announced Jesus' conception by the Holy Spirit in Mary's womb (Matthew 1:20,21), he connected this to the fact that this special child would be the Savior. By the miracle of the virgin birth, Jesus was born without sin as the God-man. As the 1 Timothy passage below then shows, it was essential that Jesus be the God-man. This was necessary for him to be the mediator who would bring peace between God and man by his sacrificial death.

> Matthew 1:20,21 But after he had considered this, an angel of the Lord appeared to him in a dream and said, "Joseph son of David, do not be afraid to take Mary home as your wife, because *what is conceived in her is from the Holy Spirit.* She will give birth to a son, and you are to give him the name Jesus, because he will save his people from their sins."

1 Timothy 2:5 For there is *one God* and *one mediator* between God and men, *the man* Christ Jesus.

Paul indicates that if the miracle of Jesus' resurrection did not take place (1 Corinthians 15:14-19) our faith is meaningless; we have no forgiveness and no hope of eternal life. Jesus indicated to the disciples (John 14:2,3) how full of comfort the miracle of his ascension was for them.

1 Corinthians 15:14-19 And *if Christ has not been raised, our preaching is useless and so is your faith.* More than that, we are then found to be false witnesses about God, for we have testified about God that he raised Christ from the dead. But he did not raise him if in fact *the dead are not raised.* For if the dead are not raised, then Christ has not been raised either. And *if Christ has not been raised, your faith is futile; you are still in your sins.* Then those also *who have fallen asleep* in Christ are lost. If only for this life we have hope in Christ, we are to be pitied more than all men.

John 14:2,3 In my Father's house are many rooms; if it were not so, I would have told you. *I am going there* to prepare a place for you. And if I go and prepare a place for you, I will come back and take you to be with me that you also may be where I am.

The miracle of inspiration

Scripture teaches that God gave us his Word by the miracle of inspiration (see chapter 1). Though written by men, Scripture has no human failings such as unclarity or error because God guided the men in their writing. He not only directed the general content of what they were to say, but he also guided them in the words they used to say it.

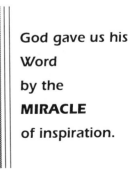

God gave us his Word by the MIRACLE of inspiration.

This supernatural act of God is also clearly taught in many passages throughout Scripture. There are the passages cited in chapter 1 (2 Peter 1:21; Hebrews 1:1; Matthew 1:22; John 14:26; 16:13,14) which state this truth directly.

There are also numerous passages that simply say God was speaking when the Old Testament prophet or the New Testament apostle said or wrote something. To give just a few examples among many, think of how often Matthew says, "This took place to fulfill what the Lord had said [or, what was said] *through the prophet . . ."* (Matthew 1:22; 2:15,17,23; 4:14, etc.) Or note that Luke records how Peter and the people of the first congregation in Jerusalem took it for granted that it was really God who spoke through all of the Old Testament prophets:

> Acts 3:18 But this is how God fulfilled what *he had foretold through all the prophets,* saying that his Christ would suffer.

> Acts 3:21 He must remain in heaven until the time comes for God to restore everything, as *he promised* long ago *through his holy prophets.*

> Acts 4:25 *You spoke by the Holy Spirit through the mouth* of your servant, our father David: "Why do the nations rage and the peoples plot in vain?"

Paul and Peter emphasize that the same is true of what the apostles said and wrote as God's messengers:

> 1 Corinthians 2:12,13 We have not received the spirit of the world but the Spirit who is from God, that we may understand what God has freely given us. This is what we speak, not in words taught us by human wisdom but *in words taught by the Spirit,* expressing spiritual truths in spiritual words.

> 2 Peter 3:2,15 I want you to recall the words spoken in the past by the holy prophets and the command *given by our Lord and Savior through your apostles. . . .* Bear in mind that our Lord's patience means salvation, just as our dear brother *Paul also wrote you with the wisdom that God gave him.*

This supernatural act of God is not an insignificant part of our Christian faith. Verbal inspiration assures us of some very important facts about the Bible:

> 1. Faith can rest its hope on all the promises it contains because God stands behind every one of these promises.

2. Its words are the basis by which true doctrine can be established and taught, and all error can be identified and rejected.

3. When we read or teach it, God convicts us of sin and leads us to despair of our own merit or works.

4. When we read or teach it, the power of the Holy Spirit is at work to bring us to faith and salvation.

Conversely, if the Bible is man's word in any way, all four of these points are rendered meaningless. If God is not speaking to us in every word of the Bible, then how can faith be certain whether all of its promises are true or not? Then how can we be sure which teachings it contains are truth and which are error? How will its messages of law and gospel speak to us with any conviction, or how can we teach these messages to others with conviction, if we're not sure whether these messages are truly God's messages or not?

Summary

Whoever denies or questions the supernatural is sure to misinterpret the Bible for three reasons:

1. He will fail to see that the central message of the Bible is God's plan of salvation because he will deny or question that God directs events in this world with one goal in mind, namely, to carry out his saving plan.

2. He will never understand Christ's person or work correctly because he will deny or question either the miracles Jesus did or the miracles that are an integral part of his work of salvation.

3. He will deny or question part or all of what the Bible teaches because he denies or questions the divine nature of Scripture.

Only the believer who knows and accepts the fact that God is almighty, that God has done and continues to do many things by his power, can rightly interpret the Bible. This is true because the only worldview of Scripture is the supernatural.

BIBLIOGRAPHY—CHAPTER THREE

Garrett, D. A., and R. R. Melick. *Authority and Interpretation.* Grand Rapids: Baker Book House, 1987.

Lawrenz, C. J. (ed.). *This Steadfast Word.* Lutheran Free Conference Publications, 1965.

4

THE ONLY TEXT THAT IS
DETERMINATIVE IS THE ORIGINAL

**The necessity for the study of the copying
of the New Testament text**

If we still had the autographs (original documents) of the
27 New Testament books today, the study of the copying of
the New Testament text would not be necessary. But God has
chosen, for reasons known only to him, to preserve his
inspired Word in copies made from the autographs instead of
preserving the autographs themselves.

This does not mean that we have any doubts about what
the original documents of the New Testament books said. Perhaps an example will illustrate why this is true. The study of
the New Testament text is not as simple as this example, but
it will help demonstrate what this chapter is all about.

Let's say a person had a ten-page document that he had 30
people copy while he read it to them. If he then lost the original document, would it be possible to restore what the original
said? Yes, it would. All one would have to do is find as many
of the 30 copies as possible and compare them with each
other. If only ten were found, the original could still be
restored by comparing these ten copies with each other.

There probably would be a few differences between the ten copies, but they would be minor things like a slight rearrangement of words, a word spelled differently, a word omitted or added, etc. But in each case, only one or two of the copies would be different from all the others in a given sentence. Obviously, one would consider the wording that the majority of the copies had (the eight or nine copies) to be what the original document said rather than the minority (the one or two copies). There would be a question about the original only if there was a fairly even split between the copies (e.g., six with one wording and four with the other wording).

The fact is that there are many more copies of the New Testament text from the early centuries of the church than there are copies of any other literature from that time. Because of these many copies, less than one percent of the text of the New Testament requires any special study.

Some people feel that to suggest that even one percent of the text needs study is tantamount to a denial of verbal inspiration. But we really don't have any choice in the matter. God didn't preserve the original copies for us. They were lost or perhaps they deteriorated with age. All that we have are copies made by hand over a number of centuries. That's just the way it is.

> **The NT text study deals with variants, not with guesses about what the original text might have been.**

Making a choice in variants

In the passages that involve the one percent of the text that needs study, the problem is not that we don't have any idea what the original wording was in the autograph. Instead, when we look at the copies of the New Testament text that we have from the early centuries of the church, some have one wording and others have a different wording (a variant). What has to be done is to make a decision between the different wordings in a variant as to which wording is the original.

In this way the study of the New Testament text is different from the study of the texts of classical Greek literature.

The latter often involves dealing with a gap or a hole in the text for which there are no other copies to suggest what is missing. That is not a problem in the study of the New Testament text.

The study of the New Testament text and the doctrines of Scripture

Before we consider how a decision is made when there is a variant, it is important to note one fact. In the passages of the one percent of the text that require a study of variants, none of the passages are ones which affect any doctrine of Scripture. So no matter which wording in a variant retains the autograph, no doctrine of Scripture is changed or altered in any way.

This does not mean that we are careless as we seek to determine what the autograph said in those few passages that have a variant. Even though it is not going to change any doctrine, we are still dealing with God's Word. Our love for every syllable of the Bible compels us to do any study of variants with the utmost care.

Two faulty approaches

Two faulty approaches have been suggested as to how one can decide which wording in a variant is the original. These two approaches have chosen to take the total number of witnesses to the New Testament and divide them into parts. Each approach then calls its chosen part the "best witnesses." This is unfortunate because each approach then bases its decision about a variant on only a part of the evidence instead of using all the evidence that God has preserved for us.

Any method that uses only part of the evidence God has preserved for us is a faulty approach.

In these approaches, the New Testament manuscripts are divided into three text-types. A text-type is a group of manuscripts that are assumed to be related because they are similar in some ways to the others in that group. But the theory that there are only three text-types has a serious problem. Manuscripts in one group are not only similar to each other but often similar to manuscripts in one of the other groups as well. When the lines that separate one group from another are drawn more strictly, the number of groups has to be expanded to several dozen. This is more than a minor problem for a theory that is dependent on the idea there are only three text-types.

In one approach, the proponents say that the Byzantine text-type is the purest form of the New Testament text and is almost always to be preferred over the Western or Alexandrian text-types. Opposed to this view are those who call the Alexandrian text-type the purest form of the New Testament text and almost always prefer it to the Western and Byzantine text-types.

When one looks at the part of the New Testament manuscripts that each approach chooses to use, the faulty nature of both approaches becomes even more evident. Those who prefer the Byzantine text-type do have almost half of the New Testament witnesses on their side. However, none of these date from the early centuries. Those who prefer the Alexandrian text-type have most of the early uncials (manuscripts written in capital letters) and the *papyri* (manuscripts written on a material made from papyrus) on their side. However, the uncials and papyri are only one part of the witnesses from the early centuries.

The Byzantine theory

Those who prefer the Byzantine text argue that the manuscripts they choose to use were the only ones copied after the sixth century. Therefore, they say, these manuscripts must be the ones that the church accepted as the purest. This argument totally ignores history.

It is a historical fact that copies of the Greek New Testament were not made in Europe because the bishop of Rome declared Latin to be the official language of the New Testament in Europe. So, after the sixth century, few if any copies of the Greek New Testament were made in Europe.

It is also a historical fact that after the Islamic conquests, only Byzantium remained of all the main centers of Christianity in the eastern Mediterranean area. After the sixth century, therefore, Byzantium was the only place in the eastern Mediterranean area where copies of the Greek New Testament were being made. This is the reason why Byzantine manuscripts were the only ones being copied through the Middle Ages. The reason was not that they were the purest manuscripts, as those who hold to the Byzantine text theory argue.

> **The Byzantine text was the only one copied after the sixth century because Byzantium was the only place where copies were being made.**

The Alexandrian theory

Those who prefer the Alexandrian text-type say that all three text-types mentioned earlier came about as the result of recensions. A recension is the supposed result of a deliberate reworking of the New Testament by an editor.

Reworking became necessary, they say, because for several centuries there was no idea in the church that the New Testament was a divinely inspired book. As a result, there was, supposedly, a rather loose handling of the Greek New Testament text. Those who made copies of the New Testament were said to have added to, excised, or altered the text as they saw fit. Finally, there were so many variants in the text that people were confused about what the New Testament really said.

To end this confusion, the leaders in at least two areas of the church agreed that an editor should put together a reworking of the text that would produce one official text of the New Testament for use in that part of the church. The official texts (which this theory says developed in Egypt and Syria) are called recensions. The Alexandrian and Byzantine text-types in turn are said to be a reflection of these recensions. Not much is said about how the Western text-type supposedly came into existence.

This recension theory is not based on historical evidence either. First, there is no record that the men who are suggested as possible recensors (Origen, Lucian, Hesychius) ever did a reworking of the New Testament text. Secondly, there is no record of any New Testament recension ever taking place in any part of the early church. It is inconceivable that this would never be mentioned in the rather detailed history of the early church we have from various sources. It is inconceivable that such an important event as a revision of the church's Bible would have taken place without anyone saying a single word about it.

> There is no historical evidence that something like recensions ever took place.

Surely such a momentous event as a reworking of the sacred text would have been noted by at least one of the early church fathers in their many writings. Why is this theory put forth in spite of such a serious lack of a historical base? Simply because the recension theory fits so well with the historical-critical view of the development of the New Testament. Therefore, it continues to remain popular among many scholars even though it has no basis for fact in history.

A suggested approach

Those who follow the recension theory generally prefer the Alexandrian witnesses, but this does not mean we ought to reject the evidence of the Egyptian uncials and papyri—as many of the Byzantine party do. Nor should we write off the Byzantine witnesses because they are later evidence—as many of the Alexandrian party do. Rather than getting locked into only one part of the manuscripts as the "best witnesses," we would do well to use all the evidence God has preserved for us. The only way to be objective is to study any and all

> An objective study of variants in the NT text will use all the evidence that God preserved for us.

variants of the text on the basis of all the evidence God preserved for us without any biases for one portion of the evidence against the rest of the witnesses.

It is impossible in this short chapter to take up all the witnesses to the New Testament text in detail. Likewise, there is much more that needs to be said about the matter of copying the text than can be presented here (e.g., the materials and methods used, the kinds of errors that came about during 1,400 years of hand copying).

Nor will the suggested method of objective text study be presented at any great length. Rather, the general guidelines will be stated and briefly explained. Details of why this method is preferred and how it is practiced are presented in a separate treatment of textual criticism, *The History and Practice of New Testament Textual Criticism* (Mequon, WI: Wisconsin Lutheran Seminary Press, 1994).

Facts about hand copying

The books of the New Testament were copied by hand for more than 1,400 years prior to the invention of the printing press in the 15th century. As a result, variants inevitably came into the text. A variant happened when a copyist's hand or eye or ear led him to write something other than what was contained in the text he was using to make a copy of all or part of the New Testament.

Most of those who made copies did so very carefully, out of respect for the Word of God. But anyone who has tried to copy something by hand knows how easy it is to make some minor mistakes. This was also true of those who worked day after day, often for hours at a time, making copies of the New Testament. In spite of great care, their hands at times wrote something slightly different from what their brains were thinking, their eyes sometimes read something slightly different from what was written on the page in front of them, or their ears heard some-

> **Anyone who has tried to copy something by hand knows how easy it is to make some minor mistakes.**

thing slightly different from what was being read to them. Copies were often made as one person read aloud while a number of people around him copied down what they heard. In this way a dozen or more copies could be made at the same time.

Remember three things: (1) We do not have any of the original documents of the New Testament books; (2) All of the "witnesses" to the New Testament text that we have contain variants, which came about through hand copying; and (3) God has preserved so many "witnesses" for us that by comparing them we can easily determine what the original documents said—except for a few passages that are not doctrinally significant.

The many witnesses we have to the New Testament text

The witnesses we have fall into two basic groups:

A. Greek manuscripts and Greek quotations

   1. Papyri = less than one hundred copies made in capital Greek letters on papyrus from A.D. 100-400.

   2. Uncials = several hundred copies made in capital Greek letters mostly on parchment from A.D. 300-900.

   3. Minuscules = several thousand copies made in small Greek letters on parchment from A.D. 800-1500.

   4. Lectionaries = several thousand copies made in small Greek letters on parchment from A.D. 800-1500.

   5. Church Fathers = quotations found in the writings of church leaders in the first six centuries after Christ.

B. Translations = several thousand copies in a number of languages: Latin (Europe and North Africa), Syriac, Coptic (Egypt), Gothic (Southeast Europe), Ethiopic, Georgian, etc.

Two guidelines for the study of New Testament variants

The two guidelines for working with variants in these witnesses are these:

1. Look at the textual evidence provided by the witnesses. The wording which is most *ancient* and most *widespread* is the one which retains the autograph. (the external evidence)

This guideline is based on the assumption that the wording that retains the autograph: (a) will be in most of the early witnesses; and (b) will be used throughout most of the early church. If the wording does not occur in the early witnesses, or if it occurs in the witnesses of only a small part of the early church, it most likely is the result of a copying error.

ANCIENT and WIDESPREAD

At the end of this chapter is a chart listing the witnesses from the first six centuries (ancient) according to regions (widespread). Using this chart will help determine which wording in a variant is the most ancient and most widespread.

2. Consider the variants in the light of the context, the author's usage, and the possibilities of an error or alteration made by the person who did the copying. (the internal evidence)

The textual evidence of the witnesses sometimes is inconclusive because neither wording of a variant is clearly more ancient and widespread than the other. This is the result of a copyist's error becoming as widespread as the autograph. In this case, the things mentioned in this second guideline must be considered in order to determine the autograph.

Sometimes in reading a letter sent to us, we have to study the letter closely to determine what a certain sentence means. The writer may not have proofread the letter, so a word or two may not make sense to us. In this case we have to establish for ourselves what the writer meant to say. We begin making this judgment by considering the immediate context in which the problem occurs. We might also compare this

CONTEXT and AUTHOR'S USAGE

sentence with another part of the letter where the same word or the same thought was used in a similar context.

In the same way, the Bible interpreter will carefully consider which wording of a variant best fits the immediate context in which the problem occurs. He will also compare this passage with any other place in the context where the author used the same word or thought in a similar way.

However, before the interpreter adopts the variant that seems to fit best with the context and the author's usage, he must consider one more thing. Might the person who did the copying have made an error because of similar words used in the context or elsewhere in Scripture? May this similarity to another passage have caused him to mistakenly alter a passage in some small way without meaning to do so?

An ERROR or ALTERATION made by the person doing the copying

Or might one of the wordings in a variant fit better because a copyist knowingly altered the text to remove what may have seemed to him to be a difficulty? Might the copyist have altered the text purposely or inadvertently to make the passage in question correspond better to a similar passage elsewhere in Scripture? In such a case the more difficult or the dissimilar reading may be preferred.

It is obvious that using the second guideline moves the interpreter into the realm of subjective considerations. That is why this second guideline should not be used until the objective evidence of the first guideline has been thoroughly investigated. Even if the objective evidence of the witnesses is not conclusive, it will usually lead the interpreter to favor one of the wordings of a variant over the other because that wording is slightly more widespread than the other. In most instances, further examination of the problem in the light of one or more of the three considerations of internal evidence in the second guideline will not change the conclusion. Almost always the latter will confirm that the wording toward which the objective evidence pointed as the autograph is the preferred wording.

Summary

Because the inspired words of the New Testament are preserved for us in copies of the autographs, it is necessary for the

New Testament Manuscripts

	North Africa	Italy Gaul	Asia Minor	Syria	Palestine	Egypt
Uncials		D	A (Gospels) W (Mt)	A (Gospels) W (Mt)	W (Mk)	Aleph, B, C, A
Minuscules			Byz	Byz		
Papyri						p^{45} p^{46} p^{47} p^{66} p^{75}
Versions	it^k it^e it^h	it^a it^b it^d vg	goth	syr^s syr^c syr^p syr^h arm	geo	cop^{sa} cop^{bo}
Lectionaries			Lect	Lect		
Church Fathers	Cyprian Tertullian (Alex) Augustine	Clement / Marcion Justin Novatian Tatian Hippolytus Hilary Ambrose Irenaeus	Papias (Rome) / Basil Gregory	Ignatius Polycarp / Eustathius Ephraem Apollinaris Chrsostom	Origen Theophilus / Eusebius Jerome	Clement Pamphilus / Origen Dionysius Alexander Athansius Arius Cyril
Early Christian Literature		Didache		Diatessaron		

interpreter to make a study of the wordings of a variant. In determining which wording retains the autograph, the interpreter should use all the objective external evidence that God has preserved for him. If this evidence of the witnesses is inconclusive, the interpreter will also consider several items of internal evidence before making a decision. Making sure that he is using the original wording is important to the interpreter because the only text that is determinative is the autograph.

BIBLIOGRAPHY—CHAPTER FOUR

Black, D. A. *New Testament Textual Criticism—A Concise Guide.* Grand Rapids: Baker Book House, 1994.

Finegan, J. *Encountering New Testament Manuscripts.* Grand Rapids: William B. Eerdmans Publishing Co., 1974. pp. 54-81.

Sturz, H. A. *The Byzantine Text-type and New Testament Textual Criticism.* Nashville: Thomas Nelson Publishers, 1984. pp. 9-49.

5

THE ONLY LITERARY CRITICISM TO BE DONE IS THE EXTERNAL KIND: THE HISTORICAL SETTING

History is an important part of the Bible record

The Bible is not meant to be a general history book. However, that does not mean that the history it records is inaccurate or that its historical content is unimportant.

God chose to work out his plan of salvation in the lives of people who are part of this world and so also part of the history recorded in the Bible. In the Old Testament, God chose one nation as his covenant people. He guided the events of Israel and of other nations. He did this so that by blessing and chastening he might train Israel in preparation for that pivotal historical event—the birth of the Savior in fulfillment of God's promise.

To accomplish our redemption, the Son of God became a man and lived for 30 years in Palestine. A portion of what he said and did, especially his public ministry, is recorded for us. It is significant that the key events in the history of all mankind, Christ's passion and resurrection, are reported in a very detailed form for us.

Jesus assigned his disciples the work of spreading the gospel of redemption to the rest of the world. Scripture also records many facts about the men who did this work and the congregations that were formed as a result of their efforts.

As his plan of salvation unfolded through the Old Testament into the New, God chose human writers to write the Bible. He inspired them to record what he had done. He also guided them to explain the significance of these events for fallen mankind. Although the importance of this verbally inspired and inerrant record is timeless, God chose to have the writers express themselves in ways that make it necessary for us to take into account the historical setting of the Bible. Three aspects that require special attention on the interpreter's part are:

1. The writers spoke the language of the particular time and place in which they lived.

2. They wrote about concrete life situations that were, for the most part, either their own experiences or the experiences of those to whom or about whom they wrote.

3. What they wrote reflects the particular stage that God's plan of salvation had reached at the time they were writing.

The relationship of history to the Bible:

- **a record of God's saving acts**

- **recorded by people at different times and places**

History, then, has a twofold relationship to God's Word. First, Scripture relates historical events that either accompany or are a basic part of the way in which God accomplished our salvation. This first relationship of history to God's Word was the focus of attention in chapter 3. Secondly, the words of the Bible have a historical setting or background because of the way in which God chose to have his Word written down for mankind. It is this second relationship that will be the focus of attention in this chapter.

The historical setting

The historical setting of words simply means: who is speaking, to whom, where, when, and why. Sometimes the historical setting may mean little, but in other instances it may be very important. For example, if a person says, "Isn't this fire beautiful?" while he and his friends are sitting around a glowing campfire on a cool evening in the north woods, those friends might readily agree. The same words, however, might elicit shock if spoken while a group of people are standing and watching a neighbor's house go up in flames.

For this reason the Bible interpreter must concern himself with the historical setting of a passage in Scripture if he wants to do full justice to his task. But the same point that was made in chapter 3 needs to be made here also. Any historical setting that is introduced into the interpretation of a Bible passage from outside the Bible should never be used to alter or deny the simple, plain meaning of what a passage says in its scriptural context. Any such historical setting should only be used to help the interpreter understand better what the words of a passage say and mean.

Obviously, the interpreter should never subjectively manufacture a historical background in order to give the words a meaning that suits him best. Nor will he ignore the historical setting if it gives a meaning that is not to his liking. Modern scholarship often does both. Tampering with the text in either of these ways is not proper interpretation. Rather, it is an unbelieving twisting of Scripture.

The historical setting provided by Scripture itself

A good deal of Scripture study needs to be done by the interpreter in order to give the historical setting its due. The interpreter needs to acquaint himself with any and all of the historical background that Scripture itself supplies. In fact, this is a must for the interpreter's work because this is information that God himself supplies about his Word as part of the inspired record.

We know only a little about the historical setting for some books of the Bible. For example, we know nothing about the book of Hebrews except that it was written to Jews sometime

> **The historical setting provided by the Bible is extremely important because it is provided by God himself.**

between Christ's death and the destruction of Jerusalem in A.D. 70. In such instances where God did not see fit to give us much information, we know that the historical setting is not all that vital to our understanding of the book.

In other instances Scripture tells us quite a bit about the historical setting. For example, for the letter to the Philippians, we know a good deal about the author, quite a bit about the recipients, and also some things about the where, when, and why of the letter. Such information should not be treated as mere window dressing. Instead, the interpreter should acquaint himself thoroughly with this information and use it properly as the background for his interpretation of the thoughts expressed in the letter.

The interpreter also needs to acquaint himself with people, places, events, customs, and so forth, that are mentioned in the Bible but not explained by Scripture itself. To do this he will search secular books on history, geography, and customs of the time. However, in using such extra-biblical books the interpreter needs to make sure that the information he is getting is not what someone has manufactured to make a passage mean what that person wants it to mean. Only that which is objective, factual information can be used by the Bible interpreter as historical background. And it should be used only to help the interpreter understand the evident meaning of the passage. It should not be used to alter or deny that meaning.

Know the author or the person quoted

Sometimes Scripture gives us a wealth of information about the author of a book. Think, for example, of all we know about the lives of Moses and Paul.

Information about the author, such as the circumstances of his life, his age, and his frame of mind, will be helpful for the interpretation of what he wrote. To know that Amos and David were shepherds explains their use of similes involving the care of sheep. We know that Peter's words in the book of Acts were spoken when his work as an apostle was just beginning and that his two epistles were written very near the end of his life. This explains, in part, the differences in emphasis and content between Peter's words in Acts and in his epistles.

THE AUTHOR

- **his personal circumstances**
- **his purpose in writing**
- **the time and place**

To know the setting of Galatians explains Paul's deep disappointment as it is expressed in chapter 1 and again in chapter 4. To know the setting of Philippians explains the great joy he expresses in chapter 1. Knowing the difference between the settings of Galatians and Philippians also helps us appreciate why there is such a difference in tone between these two books that are written by the same author.

Another important part of the historical setting is an acquaintance with the purpose for which an author wrote his book or why a person made the statement he did. To know the difference between the purposes of John's gospel and John's Revelation is a necessary first step in the right interpretation of each. To know the differences in the purposes of the synoptic gospels is a major step in the solution of why they are not only similar but also different. To know the settings of the temple cleansings by Jesus helps put his harsh words and actions into a proper perspective.

Knowing the time and place of the author's writing is also helpful. This is true, for example, in connection with the Pauline epistles. The book of Acts gives some general background in this regard. Considering Paul's remarks in his various letters in the light of what Acts tells us is profitable for the interpretation of both Acts and each of these letters.

Know the people to whom or about whom the words were written

People who are mentioned in Scripture or to whom words are addressed also need to be studied. The more the interpreter knows about these people the better he will understand their actions and the words written to them or about them.

The social situation of biblical people may be important. For example, Ruth was a Moabitess (Ruth 1:4); Onesimus, a slave (Philemon 16). Knowing what it meant to be a Gentile woman living as a widow in Israel gives an added dimension of beauty to Ruth's words spoken to Naomi (Ruth 1:16,17).

Situations that may be important as background to what a passage says & means:

- **social**
- **cultural**
- **economic**
- **educational**
- **religious**
- **political**
- **geographical**
- **agricultural**
- **personal**

Knowing the usual punishment for a runaway slave in the Roman Empire is important background for Paul's words addressed to Philemon regarding his treatment of Onesimus (Philemon 17,18).

An acquaintance with the cultural situation often gives added insight into the meaning of a passage. Washing a guest's feet on his arrival at one's home, offering him some oil for his hands and face, and greeting him with a kiss were considered common courtesies. This fact gives added poignancy to Jesus' words at the home of Simon the Pharisee (Luke 7:44-50). Knowing the funeral custom of friends and relatives gathering at the home of the deceased and carrying on with constant wailing helps us understand Jesus' words at the home of Jairus (Luke 8:52). A knowledge of wedding customs helps us follow Jesus' actions at the wedding of Cana (John 2) and the key point he makes in several parables that involve weddings.

The economic situation may be important. We know about the sufferings the Christians underwent in Macedonia (1 Thessalonians 2:14; 2 Corinthians 8:2) and their deep poverty (2 Corinthians 2:8) in contrast to the prosperity of the Christians in Corinth. This helps us understand why Paul spoke as he did in 1 and 2 Corinthians (1 Corinthians 16:1-4; 2 Corinthians 8,9) in regard to the grace of Christian giving.

The educational situation may be important background to know. The Athenians lived in a famous university town. This helps in reading Paul's words to the Athenians in Acts 17. The Galileans were known as the backward hillbillies of Palestine. That gives us a better understanding of Nathanael's words in John 1:46.

It may be essential to know the religious situation. What were the religious beliefs of the Pharisees? What kind of gods were Baal and Ashteroth? What new, but not real, gospel were the Judaizers teaching in Galatia (Galatians 1:6-24)? Answers to these questions are essential for the reader of the gospels, numerous Old Testament books, and Galatians.

Knowing the political situation is important in reading many books of the Bible. Joseph's position as Pharaoh's right-hand man in Egypt, the divided kingdom at the time of the prophets, Daniel's position in the Chaldean and Persian governments, Paul's rights as a Roman citizen—these are only a few examples.

The names of towns, mountains, rivers, plains, and so on, abound in Scripture. Often the reader may miss the full significance of passages if he does not have an acquaintance with the geographic situation in which people lived or where events took place.

Knowing the agricultural situation can be essential. The people in Israel were either involved in agriculture or were well acquainted with the raising of fruits and grains and the shepherding of herds of animals. References to these agricultural items are often made in the form of similes to explain spiritual truths. The morning dew and the olive tree are also referred to frequently because they were an important part of everyday life. Olives provided oil for their lamps, the "lotion" for their sun-dried skin, and the "butter" for their bread. The dew provided the daily moisture needed for the growing crops.

The personal situation of people in regard to one another forms another important setting for some words of Scripture. Take, for example, the relationship of David to Jonathan, or of Paul to the Philippians from whom alone he accepted financial help.

There may be other settings which are not mentioned here. The point of all those that are presented could be summarized in this way: The Bible reader (interpreter) must acquaint himself with all that can be known about the special circumstances of the person or people about whom portions of Scripture are written or to whom they are addressed. This information is often a key to fully and rightly understanding what the words of Scripture say and mean.

Know where the passage occurs
in the development of God's plan of salvation

Whether a biblical statement or event is found in the Old Testament or the New Testament can be very important. For example, the laws about food and worship that are part of the Sinaitic covenant applied only in Old Testament times. They were restrictions that were meant to keep Israel separate from other nations until the Savior came. Some of the religious laws were types which gave God's people a clear picture of what the Savior would do to save them from sin when he came. These laws lost all their validity and meaning when Christ, the antitype and the fulfillment of the Old Testament covenant, completed his work.

It is important to note the time when a statement or event took place in the development of God's plan of salvation.

Whether a passage is found early in the Old Testament history or closer to the birth of Christ may be quite significant also. Genesis 3:15 and Isaiah 53 both speak of the promised Savior, so their general sense is the same. But the interpreter would be remiss if he did not consider the added dimension that is given to each by the unique time in which it was spoken. One was spoken at the beginning of time; the other, only a few hundred years prior to when Christ came.

Likewise, the statements made by Jesus to his disciples in the gospels must be understood as being spoken at a time when his work of redemption was not yet complete. The statements of the apostles in the epistles, on the other hand, follow Christ's death and resurrection and Pentecost. These intervening events are helpful in understanding why many of the statements took the form they did.

Summary

To ignore the historical setting of the words of Scripture is to ignore the background into which God chose to place the writing of his Word. To study the historical setting and understand the words of Scripture in the light of this background is basic for the proper understanding of many biblical passages.

This is merely an application to Scripture of a principle that applies to the interpretation of any literature. The Bible interpreter does not study the historical setting in order to alter or change what Scripture says. Rather, he studies it only that he might understand both fully and rightly what the inspired author has written. Since the latter is the only legitimate use of the historical setting, the only literary criticism to be done is the external kind.

BIBLIOGRAPHY—CHAPTER FIVE

Larkin, W. J., Jr. *Culture and Biblical Hermeneutics.* Grand Rapids: Baker Book House, 1988.

Mickelsen, A. B. *Interpreting The Bible.* Grand Rapids: William B. Eerdmans Publishing Co., 1972. Chapter 7, "History and Culture," pp. 159-176.

Surburg, Raymond. *The Principles of Biblical Interpretation.* Fort Wayne: Concordia Theological Seminary Press, 1984. Chapter 11, "The Interpreter and the Historical and Cultural Background," pp. 187-211.

Zuck, R. B. *Basic Bible Interpretation.* Wheaton, IL: Victor Books, 1991. Chapter 4, "Bridging the Cultural Gap," pp. 76-97.

6

THE ONLY MEANING OF THE WORDS IS THE SIMPLE, PLAIN MEANING: THE GRAMMATICAL SETTING

Common usage

When communication takes place, the words used must be understood only according to the one obvious sense that they convey in common usage. For example, the newspaper might report that the president of our country is going to visit England and that while he is there he will see the queen. We do not have the right to decide that "England" stands for Boston and that "queen" stands for the leader of the women's liberation movement, and that, therefore, what the newspaper report really wants to say to us is that the president is going to Boston and will see the leader of the women's liberation movement while he is there. We have no right to change what the newspaper wants to communicate to us into something that we subjectively decide we want to hear, or what we in our imagination think the newspaper wants to say to us.

What is self-evident in ordinary everyday communication does not change when we read the words of God's communication to us in the Bible. Here, too, the same principle applies.

> **The only way that words can be a reliable form of communication is if they are understood according to the one simple, plain meaning they have in common usage.**

The inspired words of Scripture must be understood only according to the one obvious sense that they convey in common usage. Otherwise what God wants to communicate to us through these words is not what *he* wants to say to us but what *we* decide we want to hear him say to us.

If words have more than one meaning at the same time, if words were always double entendres, then communication in words would always be a guessing game. Normally, the simple, plain meaning of words according to common usage is the only meaning they can have. Otherwise, words would not be a reliable means of communication.

This is also true of figurative language. If a newspaper report said that the president's mind is like a steel trap, the reader would completely misunderstand if he thought that inside the president's head there was a steel trap instead of a brain. In this case the newspaper used a figure of speech, but the meaning of the words in common usage is clear, and there is but one meaning of these words.

Speaking in code and allegorizing

In a situation such as the sending of messages in a naval battle from one ship to another, communication will take place in a secret code. In using code, the two people involved agree not to use words in their simple, plain meaning. Instead, the real meaning of the message is found only by decoding the words. Apart from such a circumstance, words must mean what they say; otherwise intelligible communication would be impossible.

Allegorizing (i.e., understanding words in a sense other than their normal sense) is an illegitimate handling of spoken or written words because the person reading or hearing the words chooses to give them a different meaning without the consent of the person who wrote or spoke those words. In the example given earlier, if we capriciously choose to give a different meaning to only two words (*England* and *queen*), we change the meaning of the whole article. If we then tell someone that this is what the article said, we would completely misrepresent it.

Any allegorizing of Scripture by an interpreter is just as capricious and misleading. In chapter 8 the following example, along with others, will be given of how the Bible is often allegorized. The incident of Abraham's servant meeting Rebekah at the well (Genesis 24:16,17) is allegorized to mean that if the Christian (Abraham's servant) wishes to meet Christ (Rebekah), he must do so at the well of God's Word. This is not false doctrine, but it surely is not what Moses meant when he wrote these words in relating this event.

Those who allegorize will argue that there has to be more to the words, at least in some passages, than their simple, plain meaning. However, when the sense of words in their common usage does not yield as lofty or as edifying a message as some people would like, they do not have the right to toy with the words and give them a different meaning. That is not letting God communicate to us what he wants to say. Instead, it is people deciding for themselves what they want to hear.

The words of Scripture are clear

The words of Scripture are not written in a code that needs to be declassified by some code experts. Rather, the words of Scripture have a simple, plain meaning, which is able to make a child wise for salvation (2 Timothy 3:15). In the psalms, the point is made a number of times that one does not 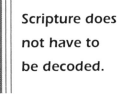 **Scripture does not have to be decoded.** need to be a scholar to read and understand God's Word:

> Psalm 19:7 The statutes of the LORD are trustworthy, *making wise the simple.*

> Psalm 119:130 The unfolding of your words gives light; it *gives understanding to the simple.*

The Bible can make a child wise and give understanding to the simple because the meaning of its words is that which is conveyed by common usage. Thus, Scripture has an objective clarity in all that it says. We might fail to grasp the one intended sense because of our sinful nature, which may blind us to a truth. Or, our weak faith and understanding might be the problem. The meaning of a passage may also go beyond our understanding because it is a miracle. Miracles by definition are events that transcend human understanding.

But if one fails to grasp the one intended sense, there is one thing that this failure does not give him the right to do. It does not give him the license to deny the clarity of Scripture and then give the words a different meaning.

Application is not giving words another meaning

Sometimes the thought is expressed that the application of Scripture seems like allegorizing. If one is not careful, one could easily slip into allegorizing (some call it "spiritualizing") in the application of a text. For example, a sermon book might suggest that the raising of Lazarus from the dead is a good text to teach that God raises the sinner from the death of unbelief to the life of faith, or that Jesus' healing of a leper shows us how Christ cleanses us from the leprosy of sin.

However, if we remember that the words of Scripture have one simple plain meaning, we realize that we cannot make the application of the raising of Lazarus one of spiritual quickening or the application of the healing of the leper one of spiritual renewing. These miracles are not speaking of the spiritual miracle of Lazarus or the leper being brought to faith. Both of these miracles speak of physical acts of healing. Thus they tell us that Jesus is true God and has divine power that enables him to raise the physically dead to life and to heal the physically sick, even the terminally ill. Our application, then, will point to Jesus as both true God and true man, and also to his power to raise us from the dead at the Last Day or to his power to heal our illnesses if he knows this is best for us.

"SPIRITUALIZING' is never proper application.

If a person wants to use the raising of a body from the dead or the healing of blind eyes as a picture of a person coming to faith, he should go to those passages in Scripture where that is the simple, plain meaning of the words in that passage:

> Ephesians 2:4,5 God, who is rich in mercy, *made us alive with Christ even when we were dead in transgressions*— it is by grace you have been saved.

> Acts 26:17,18 I am sending you to them *to open their eyes* and turn them from darkness to light, and from the power of Satan to God, so that they may receive forgiveness of sins and a place among those who are sanctified by faith in me.

Finding a passage that uses leprosy as a picture of sin or the healing of a leper as a picture of the forgiveness of sins will be more difficult because Scripture never directly uses leprosy or the healing from leprosy as a picture in this way.

This is an especially important point to remember in our day when the historical-critical method is used by so many in the religious world. Those who use this method often "spiritualize" in their applications to avoid the simple, plain meaning of the words in a passage. For us to do this from time to time not only would be improper interpretation, but also could confuse people if we condemn the interpretation of the historical-critical method while doing something very similar ourselves.

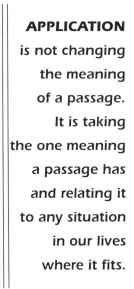

APPLICATION is not changing the meaning of a passage. It is taking the one meaning a passage has and relating it to any situation in our lives where it fits.

Proper application

Proper application of Scripture will not change the simple, plain meaning of a text in any way, but it will bring that meaning to bear on the various situations where it fits. For example, the meaning of the words "The righteous will live by faith" (Galatians 3:11) may have a number of applications. It might be applied in pointing out the crass work righteousness of Mormonism or the equally damning error of mixing faith and works as is done in Roman Catholicism. These words might be used to warn a pious Christian against the self-righteous thoughts of his own sinful flesh. Or, they might be used to comfort a Christian on his deathbed.

Each of the situations just mentioned in which this passage might be applied is quite different from the others. But, in each of these applications, the simple, plain meaning of the words is the same, namely, a person is justified in God's sight, not by works, but by faith alone.

Individual word meanings

How does the interpreter establish the simple, plain meaning of a passage in Scripture? As in the study of any language, the first step is a study of the vocabulary of that language. Determining the meaning of individual words is basic for translation and so also for interpretation.

Etymology (the history of a linguistic form) may be helpful in the study of the words of the biblical languages. Looking at the meaning of the root word or words that make up a given word can be a good memory hook on which to hang that word's meaning.

But etymology needs to be used with caution. There are hundreds of years of usage behind each of the biblical languages. The etymology of a word will give that word's original meaning, but over the centuries of use that word's meaning may have changed so that later it may have little or no relationship to the original meaning.

The father who tries to discover etymologically what his daughter means when she refers to his tie with some word like *cool* will not get very far. It may just be the current use of a word to express a thought such as "Your tie is very nice." The same is true of a person reading the sports section who wants to determine by etymology what a "rhubarb" is in a baseball game.

Similarly, the etymology of Bible words may be no help or may even be misleading. Take, for example, the Greek word *ekklesia,* which means "church," or "congregation," in the New

Testament. *Ekklesia* is made up of two words: *ek,* which means "out of," and *kaleo,* which means "to call." There was a time in early Athens when its "assembly" was a gathering of men who were "called out of" the marketplace. However, as the years went by the Athenian assembly continued to be called the *ekklesia* even after the men were no longer being called out of the marketplace.

It was in this later sense (of simply referring to people assembled in a group) that this word was used in the Septuagint to translate the Hebrew word *kahal* (congregation). The New Testament usage reflects the later Greek usage and the Septuagint usage. The Bible interpreter who goes back to the etymological meaning of *ekklesia* and says that it means those who have been "called out of" the unbelieving world to faith in Christ is not accurately reflecting the meaning of this word in the common usage of New Testament times. Therefore, in his interpretation of a verse, he will be stating something about the meaning of this word that really isn't true.

On the other hand, there are words whose usage coincides with their etymology. The Greek verb *aphiemi* means etymologically "to send away." In the New Testament it is often used with the meaning "to forgive." In this case the interpreter can and should use the etymological meaning because it provides a vivid picture of what the word forgive means: God takes our sins from us and sends them far away—as Psalm 103:12 says, "as far as the east is from the west."

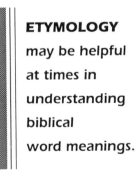

ETYMOLOGY may be helpful at times in understanding biblical word meanings.

Sometimes a word is used only once in all of the Greek or Hebrew literature that we have. Obviously, in such a case the etymology of that word is the only way the interpreter has to try to determine its meaning. The word *pistikos* in Mark 14:3 is an example. The NIV translates this verse: "A woman came with an alabaster jar of very expensive perfume, made of *pure* nard." Some suggest that the italicized word comes from the word *pino* and so translate it "liquid." Others suggest that it comes from *pistis* and translate it as the NIV does with "pure." Still others suggest that it has something to do with the picita plant of India and so is a nard made from this plant. We finally have to admit that we are not sure what the word means exactly, but etymology does make it possible for us to make some educated guesses.

Etymology may be helpful, then, but it should never be used to set aside or alter the meaning of a word as it has been established by usage.

Word usage

The best way to determine word meaning is to look at the meaning of that word as established by usage. In doing this, the immediate context must always take precedence over any wider biblical usage. For example, the word *soteria* is usually used in the New Testament to mean "salvation" in the spiritual sense. But in Acts 27:34 there is no doubt that in this context Paul is using it to refer to a purely physical salvation, namely, escape from drowning. The usual use of this word in the rest of the New Testament does not determine its meaning in this passage. Here the immediate context takes precedence over the rest of the New Testament usage.

> **WORD USAGE is the definitive way of establishing word meanings.**

Some words are used in the Bible with two different meanings or a number of different shadings in meaning. How does the interpreter handle passages where such words occur? There are two basic guidelines: (1) The interpreter must study a word's full range of meaning as determined by usage and not go beyond it on the basis of a personal whim. (2) The precise meaning in each biblical passage is determined by the immediate context, that is, the shade of meaning that the immediate context indicates the original speaker or writer meant to convey to the original audience.

For example, the Greek adjective *dikaios* in a context that is speaking of sanctification describes a person's actions as being in accord with what God declares to be the right thing to do ("righteous" in Matthew 1:19, "upright" in Luke 1:6). In a passage that is speaking of justification this adjective describes a believer's status in God's courtroom—free of all blame as a result of Jesus' redemptive work ("righteous" in Galatians 3:11).

> Matthew 1:19 Because Joseph her husband was a *righteous* man and did not want to expose her to public disgrace, he had in mind to divorce her quietly.

> Luke 1:6 Both of them were *upright* in the sight of God, observing all the Lord's commandments and regulations blamelessly.

> Galatians 3:11 Clearly no one is justified before God by the law, because, "The *righteous* will live by faith."

Note that if the context is one of sanctification, the meaning of this same word is quite different from what it means if the context is one of justification.

This also helps illustrate the fact that not every passage in which a word occurs is a parallel usage. The interpreter must be sure to consider only those passages as parallel where the word is used in the same kind of immediate context.

Biblical usage in turn must take precedence over usage in non-biblical literature. The example of the Greek verb *baptizo* illustrates this. In Greek literature prior to the New Testament time, *baptizo* normally meant to sink under water. It is used of ships sinking or people drowning. But a study of the word in New Testament usage makes it clear that it is used in the wider sense of sprinkling or washing as well as of immersing. In the following passage from Mark, the italicized word is *baptizo* in Greek:

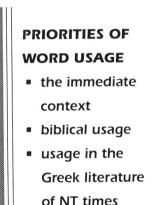

PRIORITIES OF WORD USAGE

- **the immediate context**
- **biblical usage**
- **usage in the Greek literature of NT times**

> Mark 7:3,4 The Pharisees and all the Jews do not eat unless they give their hands a ceremonial washing, holding to

> the tradition of the elders. When they come from the
> marketplace they do not eat unless they wash. And they
> observe many other traditions, such as the *washing* of
> cups, pitchers and kettles [and dining couches—NIV
> footnote].

Therefore, to insist that *baptize* means only "immerse" in the New Testament is indefensible.

Some of the special theological terms in the Bible are words that were taken from everyday use by people of biblical times. Examples are words such as "redeem" (pay a price to set a person free), "justify" (a judge declaring a person not guilty), "sin" (miss the bull's-eye at an archery range), and "transgression" (step over a forbidden line). In the Bible they are given a fuller spiritual meaning, but the everyday meaning of these words is important to remember. The everyday meaning provides a simple and concrete understanding of a word that for us has far too often become an abstract term.

Take the Greek word *apolutrosis* as an example. In its normal usage by people of biblical times, it meant the freeing of a prisoner of war, a slave, or a criminal by the payment of a ransom. In the New Testament it is usually used in the spiritual sense of the freeing of the sinner from the slavery of sin, death, and the devil by the ransom that Jesus paid by his death. English translations often use the word "redeem" for *apolutrosis*. The Bible interpreter, however, should not forget the everyday meaning this word had in the life of people of biblical times. To think of ourselves as a prisoner of war, or a slave, or a criminal who was freed by the payment of Jesus blood fills our hearts with a much deeper appreciation of what the Bible means by this word.

Synonyms

In considering individual word meanings, the interpreter must also give attention to synonyms. Often synonyms have a slight difference in meaning which needs to be taken into account, especially when synonyms are used together in the same context.

In Matthew 9:17 Jesus says that one puts new wine (Greek = *neos,* i.e., new in time) into new wineskins (Greek = *kainos,* i.e., new in quality). This helps us understand the picture Jesus is using, namely, new fermenting wine should be put into a new wineskin that will stretch as the wine ferments, otherwise the skin container will burst if it is dried out and does not stretch at all anymore. Or consider the example in John 21: Jesus switched in his third question "Do you love me?" from the word *agapao* (the love of choice or selection and so a more reasoned attachment) to the word *phileo* (the love of attraction and so an attachment of feeling). This added a poignancy which we are told hurt Peter.

Lexicons and concordances

Lexicons are a basic tool for use by the interpreter who can read the Bible in the original languages (Hebrew, Greek) because they give the meaning of biblical words based on usage. A comprehensive New Testament lexicon,[1] for example, will tell not only how a word is used in the New Testament. It will also indicate how that word was used in classical Greek, the Septuagint, the literary and non-literary Greek of New Testament times, and the early Christian literature. If a word has different meanings or shadings of the same meaning, the lexicon will give citations where the word occurs in each of these uses. This enables the interpreter to do some independent, comparative study of a word's usage to help with his interpretation of that word in a biblical passage.

The interpreter needs to maintain a healthy skepticism if a lexicon suggests an unusual meaning for a word in a biblical passage without any support for that meaning from usage either in the New Testament or in other Greek literature. Unless the meaning suggested for a passage is based on usage, it is only a guess on the part of the author(s) of the lexicon. It might be an educated guess, to be sure, but it is still only a guess. Perhaps the guess might even be prompted by the author's theological persuasion and, therefore, faulty to the degree his theology is faulty.

A good concordance[2] can also be helpful. There are Greek concordances, English concordances that give the corresponding Greek words, and just plain English concordances. All are helpful for the interpreter because they will list most, if not all, of the biblical passages in which a particular word is used. Sometimes a concordance will give the interpreter more passages to consider than those listed in the lexicons.

One final help in determining word meanings should be mentioned at least in passing, namely, the early translations of the New Testament (Syriac, Coptic, Latin, Gothic, Ethiopic, Georgian, etc.). Since they give a translation of New Testament Greek words, they indicate how those who were closer to New Testament times than we are understood the meaning of words in their context.

Syntax

The second vital step in the interpretation of any language is the study of the syntax of the biblical languages. Syntax is the study of the connection and relation of words as they are arranged grammatically. This is just as important as the study of individual word meanings. Words are arranged in the Bible from groupings of a few words to groupings of thousands of words: phrase or clause, sentence, paragraph, chapter, book. How words are arranged in these groupings also contributes to what God wants to communicate to us through his inspired Word. This point was made earlier when it was stressed that the meaning of a word according to usage in the immediate context must take precedence over its usage in the wider context of the Bible or other non-biblical literature. But the point must be emphasized again in speaking of the syntax because now we are looking at a given grouping of words according to considerations such as these:

1. The *kind of words* they are: nouns, verbs, participles, prepositions, adverbs, adjectives, pronouns, particles, conjunctions, interjections

2. The *forms they take:* verbs have tense, voice, mood, person, and number; nouns and adjectives [in Greek] have case, number, and gender

3. The *order in which they occur:* genitives are usually right after the noun they modify; the position at the

beginning or end of the sentence can be used for emphasis; unusual word order can express emphasis

4. The *way groupings of words are coordinated or subordinated* within a sentence, from sentence to sentence, from paragraph to paragraph, and even from one larger section to another

The use of grammars and commentaries

How much influence should the analysis of the syntax of a given passage of Scripture by a thorough grammar[3] or commentary have on the interpreter? Because a grammar or commentary cites a verse and explains the syntax in a certain way, the interpreter may be tempted to take this as the final word on the syntax of that verse because it is the conclusion of a well-known grammarian or theologian.

However, syntax is established by usage, not by famous grammarians or theologians. Thus a bit of skepticism toward a grammar's or a commentary's analysis is a healthy thing if what is said about the syntax of a verse is not based on usage. In such a case the grammarian's or theologian's conclusion is only a guess—an educated guess, to be sure—but still only a guess, and perhaps a guess that reflects the author's faulty theological persuasion.[4]

> **Don't accept a grammar's or a commentary's analysis of syntax unless it is clearly based on usage.**

For this reason the Bible interpreter who has studied the biblical languages needs to keep up his language skills. It is only in this way that he will be able to evaluate syntactical constructions in a way that is not totally reliant on a grammar. This last statement is doubly true in regard to commentaries because the author of a commentary will often give only his analysis of a verse without referring to other syntactical possibilities. Or, he may stack the deck with arguments that favor his understanding of the verse.

This is the reason our pastors study the biblical languages as part of their training. It is also the reason why a congregation should make sure that its pastor has time every week for private study of the Bible in its original languages. Our pastors will be able to analyze what is false interpretation and to interpret the Bible properly only to the degree that they are able to study Scripture on the basis of the original languages.

Sometimes the syntax allows two possible interpretations

What does the interpreter do if the situation arises in which the syntax allows for two different interpretations of a verse? If one of the possibilities would teach something that is contrary to a clear statement made elsewhere in Scripture, that syntactical possibility must be rejected. God does not contradict himself, and so he could not lead one of his inspired writers to make a statement that would contradict the words of another writer.[5]

If two interpretations of a verse are possible syntactically and neither contradicts the rest of Scripture, the one that best fits the context is the proper interpretation.

On the other hand, if the differing syntactical possibilities say nothing contradictory to anything else in Scripture, the interpreter will determine which one fits best in the immediate context and use that one in his interpretation of the verse.[6] He will not say that the verse has more than one meaning because every statement in Scripture, like all other written communication, has only one proper intended sense. The only exception would be if the context makes it clear that the author or speaker is using a pun or a play on words.

What happens if a fellow Christian argues that the other syntactical possibility fits better in the context of a given verse than the one I'm convinced best fits the context? Remember that it was said earlier that we are dealing here with a passage in which neither interpretation contradicts anything else in Scripture. It is unfortunate that we cannot agree on the meaning of this particular verse, but the difference of our interpretations for this verse does not have to be divisive of fellowship. Neither person is advocating something contrary to Scripture, and both in principle do not want to say anything other than what Scripture says.[7] In short, we still agree on every doctrine of Scripture. We just don't agree on which doctrine of Scripture this particular verse is referring to or teaching.

Genre

In addition to a careful study of individual word meanings and syntax, the interpreter must also identify the kind of literature in which a biblical passage is found. This is another item that determines meaning. For example, in the Bible as in any other piece of literature, poetry cannot be read as narrative and vice versa.

GENRE

- apocalypse

- poetry

- epistle

- narrative

- prophecy-
  teaching

The term that is often used to refer to the kind of literature one is reading is genre. Some genres that are clearly identified in Scripture are: apocalypse, poetry, letter (epistle), narrative, and prophecy-teaching.

Apocalypse is characterized by fantastic imagery. As one example, in the book of Revelation, Jesus is described in some very different and striking ways from one part of the book to the next. In 1:16 he is a person with a double-edged sword coming out of his mouth. In 5:6 he is a Lamb with seven horns and seven eyes. In 19:11 he is a rider on a white horse. Since there are many other passages like this in Revelation, the interpreter of Revelation can easily interpret parts of this book improperly if he does not keep in mind the special kind of literature he is reading.

Hebrew poetry is characterized by parallelism of several kinds. The second part of a line (or a second line) will explain, expand on, or contrast with the first part of the line (or the preceding line). The epistles in the New Testament have one basic format (with some omissions on occasion): introduction, thanksgiving, main body, greeting, and conclusion. To be aware of each of these kinds of structure in the poetry or epistle portions of the Bible is essential for the interpreter.

Narrative is the statement of historical data. It may take the form of law or history or biography, etc. But in each case the reader is given a report of such things as what took place, at what time, who was involved, where, and why. To take any portion of Scripture that is narrative and interpret it as figurative language is obviously not legitimate interpretation.

Prophecy-teaching is the declaration and explanation of spiritual truths (doctrine). The prophets, apostles, and evangelists declare God's will, explain it, and apply it. They declare God's judgment on the sinner, as well as God's loving grace as evidenced in his working out his plan of salvation. They declare God's providential care of the world and especially of his believing children. They invite and urge people to embrace and cling to the grace of God by faith.

Some like to turn portions of the Bible that are prophecy-teaching into poetic or figurative language. This is usually done to avoid having doctrinal passages speak with the authority of God. It is clearly improper interpretation to change the genre of any portion of Scripture at any time. It is particularly improper when this is done in order to make God say what the interpreter wants him to say instead of what God actually says.

Portions of Scripture are not always just one type of genre or another. Any book or chapter or portion of a chapter of the Bible may be a combination of two or more genres. It is quite natural that prophecy-teaching should run through all of Scripture because the basic purpose of the Bible is to teach the only way of salvation in Christ. It is also natural that narrative should form large portions of the Bible. This is true because God carried out his saving plan in the history of the world by directing historical events to serve his gracious purpose.

How does one determine the genre of any portion of Scripture? In the same way one determines the genre of any other piece of literature. Genre is determined from the immediate context or from clear references elsewhere in the document under study.

In the Bible, sometimes the context indicates the genre of a portion of Scripture. The book of Genesis is divided into toledoths (narratives). Therefore, it is clearly identified within the book itself as narrative, not poetry. The structure of the psalms, for example Psalm 23, identifies the psalms as poetry. The prophets (Jeremiah 1:17; Hosea 1:1) identify their writings as prophecy-teaching. Luke identifies his gospel as narrative in the opening words of the book of Acts. Paul (Colossians 4:16) and Peter (2 Peter 3:1) identify their writings as epistles. In the opening verse of the book of Revelation, John identifies the book as an apocalypse.

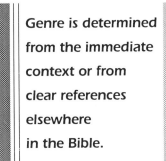

Genre is determined from the immediate context or from clear references elsewhere in the Bible.

Sometimes references in other parts of Scripture help identify or affirm the genre of portions of the Bible. The following are a few examples taken from the first chapters of the book of Acts: Acts 1:20 identifies Psalm 69 as poetry; Acts 2:16 identifies Joel 2:28-32 as prophecy-teaching; in Acts 7 Stephen identifies many Old Testament events as history.

The genre of any portion of Scripture must be identified in one of these two ways, either by the immediate context or from some clear witness elsewhere in Scripture. Genre cannot be determined subjectively in order to make a portion of the Bible fit some preconceived pattern. This is done by some whose historical-critical bias leads them to classify most, if

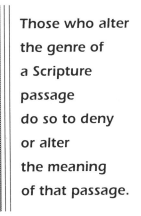

Those who alter the genre of a Scripture passage do so to deny or alter the meaning of that passage.

not all, of the New Testament as one genre, namely, the *kerygma* of the early church (see chapter 10 for an explanation of kerygma).

Scripture does not leave the interpreter in doubt as to the genre of any portion of God's Word. Those who choose to ignore this fact, or who alter Scripture's identification of the genre of any part of the Bible, do so only in order that they might deny or alter the simple, plain meaning of a passage.

Figurative language: how it is established

The interpretation of figurative language is one aspect of biblical interpretation that has caused more problems than any other. Most interpreters who have drifted away from the simple, plain meaning of biblical passages have exalted figurative language in importance and then imposed it where it does not belong. Two prime examples are the allegorizing of the Middle Ages (chapter 8) and the demythologizing of one form of the historical-critical method (chapter 10).

What is literal should not be interpreted figuratively.

What is figurative should not be interpreted literally.

But there is also the opposite mistake of failing to recognize a passage as figurative and then interpreting it literally. This can produce just as erroneous an interpretation as does the figurative interpretation of a literal passage. One of the errors of millennialists, for example, is their literal interpretation of various figurative Bible portions such as several Old Testament prophecies and selected parts of the book of Revelation.

How does the interpreter decide whether a biblical passage is literal or figurative? The decision must be based on the same criteria as in any other literature: (1) Either the writer or speaker must indicate in direct words that he is using a figure of speech; (2) Or the context must make it clear that the words have to be taken figuratively.

In any other case, the literal meaning of the words must be accepted as the intended sense.

The following are not legitimate reasons for departing from the literal sense:

1. A word or phrase makes good sense if it is understood figuratively.
2. A literal interpretation yields a sense that reason cannot grasp.
3. The literal interpretation involves difficulties that would be avoided by a figurative interpretation.
4. Some famous theologian has given a figurative interpretation for the word or phrase in question.
5. The word or phase in question is used in a figurative sense elsewhere in Scripture.

The use of figurative language

Figurative language is used by almost everyone in what they say or write, but as a general rule it is used more frequently by common people than by scholars. The scholar usually has a larger vocabulary, and so he does not have to use figures of speech as often as other people might. The uneducated person, on the other hand, often resorts to his experience to express himself. For example, the scholar may tell you that during his trip through the desert he experienced a sweltering, stifling heat. The common person, on the other hand, is more likely to tell you that the desert is like an open oven or like going up to his attic.

Figurative speech is also used because it is concrete and vivid. Therefore, it often has an emotional impact on the reader or hearer in addition to conveying something to his intellect. Television commercials regularly use figurative speech to make people feel a need for a particular product.

Scripture also uses figures of speech to make an abstract truth vivid and concrete for us. For example, the Bible teaches us the truth that God alone can make us able to live a sanctified life. The Lord (John 15:1-17) makes this truth vivid and concrete for us by using a figure of speech. Jesus calls himself the Vine and us the branches. If we remain in Jesus and Jesus remains in us, we can bear fruit. Without Jesus we can do nothing.

Another example of teaching a biblical truth abstractly would be to tell a worried or dying Christian that God is with him and will watch over him. A person could make this same point vividly with a strong emotional impact by using figurative language such as that of Psalm 23, which speaks of God as a loving and caring shepherd. "The LORD is my shepherd, I shall not be in want. . . . He leads me beside quiet waters, he restores my soul. . . . Even though I walk through the valley of the shadow of death, I will fear no evil, for you are with me; your rod and your staff, they comfort me. . . . Surely goodness and love will follow me all the days of my life, and I will dwell in the house of the LORD forever." It's easy to see why this is a favorite psalm of so many Christians. Its figurative language is so clear and so comforting.

Figurative language makes an emotional impact because it is vivid and concrete.

Since figurative language is illustrative, it is used to reveal things to people. It is not used to confuse or to conceal—as some contend Jesus did.[8] The manner in which it reveals is obvious upon observation. How did the person describe the desert to his friend who had never been there? He simply used something his friend knew, namely, an oven or an attic. He used something his friend knew about to help his friend, who had never been to a desert, get a better idea of what a desert is like. Basically, this is what most figures of speech do: they use something known to help a person understand something unknown.

Figurative language uses something known to explain something unknown.

For this reason, using figurative language is often the best way to explain something to a small child whose experiences in life are still rather limited. For example, a Sunday school teacher will not help her little children understand what the

Sea of Galilee is like by pointing to a map. However, if a large lake is nearby that she knows the children have seen, she can compare the Sea of Galilee to that lake.

God knows that we are often children as far as our spiritual understanding is concerned. Therefore, he uses figurative language throughout Scripture to communicate truths to us about his kingdom, which we could not grasp in any other way. How readily we understand the spiritual power we derive from Jesus when the Bible describes him as the Vine and us as the branches! How tenderly we can picture his loving care for us when he calls himself our Shepherd! How easily we understand many of the mysteries of his saving Word when he explains, "The kingdom of heaven is like . . ."

A problem in understanding scriptural figures of speech

Sometimes we have a problem with understanding figures of speech in Scripture. This is not because the words in the figure are hard for us to understand. Instead, the problem is that, although the figure of speech may have been known to the people at the time the Bible was written, it is not part of our experience in modern America. The item that is the "known" (which is supposed to explain the unknown to us) is something "unknown" to us. For example, the wedding customs of Jesus' day were obviously known to the people to whom Jesus spoke. But if

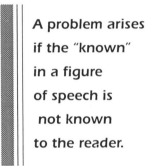

A problem arises if the "known" in a figure of speech is not known to the reader.

those customs are not known to us, we may not catch on to the point about God's kingdom that Jesus wants to teach when he uses those wedding customs as an illustration.

Since many of the figures have to do with plants and animals, people who live in rural areas today may have an advantage over urbanites in regard to some figures of speech used in Scripture. On the other hand, most of us understand the value of a beautiful pearl, or we can easily picture a net catching fish. Other biblical figures of speech, such as the following, may be less familiar to us: the kind of lamps the Jews had and the oil they put in their lamps; how small a mustard seed is and how large the mustard bush grows; the feeling of value the Jews had for sheep in contrast to the aversion they had for goats.

The interpreter must see to it that he bridges such cultural gaps so that what was used as the known in the figure of speech for people of biblical times also is known to people today. Unless the interpreter does a good job of this, people will be deprived of the help they need to understand the abstract spiritual concepts that God has chosen to explain by figurative language.

Figurative language: the point of comparison

In interpreting a figure of speech, the interpretation must be limited to the one point of comparison.

Once we fully understand the known in a figure of speech, we are ready to compare it with the unknown. This is the area in which the interpretation of figurative language can easily go wrong unless a basic principle is carefully observed. The basic principle for the interpretation of figures of speech in any language is this: *There is only one point of comparison between the known and the unknown.*

The only proper procedure for interpreting figurative language, therefore, is:

1. Identify the known in the figure of speech.
2. Identify the unknown.
3. Identify the one point of comparison (also called the tertium, the third element in a figure of speech).
4. The interpretation of the figure of speech must be limited to the one point of comparison.
5. The interpretation of details in the figure of speech must be limited to those details which develop the one point of comparison. Any interpretation of details which leads to a second point of comparison is illegitimate interpretation.

This basic principle and the procedure it requires can be illustrated by an example from everyday life. Let's say that a friend of mine had an especially tall visitor whom I don't know. My friend wishes to explain to me how tall this visitor was. He says, "You know that young pine tree in my back yard. Well, he was as tall as that tree." By referring to the tree my friend is making only one comparison, namely, how tall the visitor was. So the known is the pine tree; the unknown is the visitor; and the point of comparison he is making between the two (the tertium) is the height of the visitor.

It would be pure folly on a my part to begin to imagine that, because my friend compared the visitor's height to that of the pine tree, there are also all kinds of other points of comparison between the pine tree and the visitor. To assume that the visitor's skin was like the bark of the tree, that his fingers were like the twigs of the tree, that his legs and feet and toes were like the roots of the tree, that his clothing was dark green like the needles of the tree—all such comparisons are pure imagination on my part. They are not what my friend said or meant. To give meaning to any point other than the height of the tree would be a misuse on my part of the figure of speech used by my friend. The one point of comparison he made between the known and unknown was height. I have no right to go beyond that stated point of comparison.

What is obvious in this example must also be remembered in the interpretation of Scripture. Interpreters sometimes let their imaginations run as wild in the interpretation of parables as I might have with my friend's figure of speech if I forget his one point of comparison. In chapter 8 which follows, an example will be given of how Augustine interpreted every detail of the parable of the good Samaritan. He takes the reader from Eden to Judgment Day by comparing each of the details of this parable with events in God's plan of salvation. In the process, his interpretation ends up obliterating the real reason why Jesus told that parable, namely, to stress that a person's neighbor is anyone in need.

Likewise, the interpreter who tries to find a meaning for every detail in the parable of the ten virgins may lose sight of the one point that the parable is meant to teach. The parable does not teach how many will be saved and how many will be lost (five wise and five foolish), nor that faith is like the light of the lamp and the oil like the Word of God (the five wise also slept and their lamps went out), etc. Jesus indicates the one point of comparison he wanted the hearers to make when he said at the end of the parable, "Therefore keep watch, because you do not know the day or the hour" (Matthew 25:13).

Pulling the details of a figure of speech out of the background and trying to interpret them will do more than complicate the interpretation. Often it will also destroy the one real point that the biblical speaker or writer is making. Proper interpretation is always limited to the one point of comparison because this is the only way the simple, plain meaning of figurative language will be maintained.

In most cases, when this principle is observed, the interpretation of figures of speech in the Bible is quite simple. Sometimes the statement is made that the interpretation of figurative language in Scripture is one of the most difficult parts of biblical interpretation. Just the opposite is true. If we understand the known in the figure of speech and limit ourselves in the interpretation to the one point of comparison, those passages that have figurative language should be some of the easiest for us to interpret. In turn, they should also be some of the easiest texts to explain in sermons or Bible, Sunday school, and catechism classes.

Short figures of speech

Almost every type of figurative language that occurs in other literature is also used by the biblical writers. Many of these are short figures of speech, that is, they involve only a verse or two.

There are figures of lively presentation such as simile and metaphor. A *simile* uses an expression stating that the unknown "is like" the known. In Luke 17:24 Jesus says, "The Son of Man in his day will be like the lightning."

A *metaphor,* on the other hand, states the unknown directly in terms of the known. This brings out even more emphatically the point of comparison between the two. In Luke 13:32 Jesus is referring to King Herod when he says, "Go tell that fox . . . ," and in John 15:5 Jesus makes an emphatic comparison by saying, "I am the vine."

Figures of association such as metonomy and synecdoche are also used in the Bible. *Metonomy* is the use of one word to stand for another readily identifiable word or thought. Abraham is obviously referring to God's Word when he says, "They have Moses and the Prophets; let them listen to them" (Luke 16:29), and Paul is referring to the wine when he says, "For whenever you . . . drink this cup . . ." (1 Corinthians 11:26). *Synecdoche* uses the part to designate the whole. In Psalm 16:9 when the psalmist says, "Therefore . . . my tongue rejoices," he is referring to the joy of his whole being, which is expressed outwardly in words.

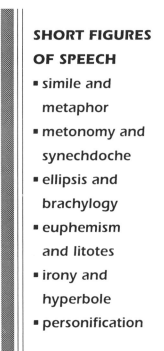

SHORT FIGURES OF SPEECH

- simile and metaphor
- metonomy and synechdoche
- ellipsis and brachylogy
- euphemism and litotes
- irony and hyperbole
- personification

Ellipsis and brachylogy are figures which are characterized by omissions. *Ellipsis* is the omission of an element necessary to the construction. In 1 Corinthians 6:13 we have to supply the verb *is* twice in the expression "Food for the stomach and the stomach for food." Brachylogy is the omission of an element necessary to the thought. In 1 John 5:9 we read, "We accept man's testimony, but God's testimony is greater because it is the testimony of God." The context leads us to add the unexpressed thought that therefore we surely also accept God's testimony.

Scripture also uses figures that soften or that emphasize. Peter used a *euphemism* to soften[9] his statement about Judas when he said in Acts 1:25, "Judas left to go where he belongs (literally: to go to his own place)." Paul emphasized God's anger by using a *litotes* to understate how God felt about the

Jews who killed Jesus and the prophets when he said in 1 Thessalonians 2:15, "They displease God."

Jesus used *irony* in Mark 7:9 to emphasize his condemnation of the Jewish leaders for their hypocritical piety by saying, "You have a fine way of setting aside the commands of God." John uses *hyperbole* in John 21:25 to emphasize his point by overstating it. He wanted his readers to realize that what was recorded in Scripture for them about Jesus' life was only a small portion of all that he said and did. So John says, "If every one of them were written down, I suppose that even the whole world would not have room for the books that would be written."

Sometimes *personification* is used in Scripture. A thing is used to represent a person in order to make a point in a vivid way. In Matthew 6:34 Jesus says, "Do not worry about tomorrow, for tomorrow will worry about itself." Sometimes a thing is also addressed as a person as Paul does in 1 Corinthians 15:55, "Where, O death, is your victory?"

Longer figures of speech: allegory and parable

An *allegory* can be described as an extended metaphor. An allegory uses the details of a historical event to teach one or more spiritual truths. Allegory is rarely used in Scripture. The only allegory in the New Testament occurs in Galatians 4:21-31. Since it is a rare use of this longer figure of speech, it is not surprising that the Holy Spirit led Paul to clearly label it as such as he began to use it.[10]

> An **ALLEGORY** is an extended metaphor; a **PARABLE** is an extended simile.

In this allegory Paul uses the historical situation in Abraham's house involving Sarah the free woman, Hagar the slave woman, and their sons. Paul points out God's solution to the problem that arose when both women bore children and the question arose regarding who was the real heir. This same problem, Paul suggests by way of the allegory, exists in Galatia. So the solution should be the same also.

A *parable* can be described as an extended simile. Since there are no absolute boundaries or literary classifications for figures of speech, the line which divides a simile from a parable may be drawn at different points by different people. But this really doesn't make any difference. The principles given earlier about the interpretation of figures of speech apply equally no matter whether a passage is identified as a simile or a parable.

As was noted earlier, the interpretation of parables is not very difficult if one remembers that each parable has one known, one unknown, and one point of comparison between the two (tertium). The tertium of a parable will be indicated either in the opening or closing words of the parable, or by the historical setting, or by the aim of the parable.

The historical setting of the parable of the good Samaritan reveals its tertium. The question that occasioned the parable ("Who is my neighbor?") and the question Jesus asked of the expert of the law at the end of the parable ("Which of these three do you think was a neighbor . . . ?") make it clear that the tertium is the fact that our neighbor is anyone who is in need of help. In the same way, the context of the parable of the wedding banquet (Matthew 22:1-14) indicates that Jesus told this parable to convict his enemies of their sin.

Interpreting the details of a parable

Earlier the point was emphasized that the interpreter must interpret the details of a parable with strict reference to the one point of comparison so that the focus remains on the one spiritual truth taught by the parable. But how many details does this mean one will use in the interpretation of a given parable? This will vary from parable to parable.

Sometimes *none of the details* of a parable will be used in the interpretation. The parable of the good Samaritan again serves as a good

Sometimes none of the details, sometimes a few of the details, sometimes all of the details of a parable are to be interpreted.

example. All of the details merely serve as background for the example of the Samaritan helping someone in need. Identifying the wine that the Samaritan poured into the injured man's wounds as the law and the olive oil as the gospel takes the parable in a totally different direction from that which Jesus intended. The same thing happens when any of the details are used as anything except background in the following parables: the unjust judge and the persistent widow (Luke 18), the lost sheep (Luke 15), the lost coin (Luke 15), the unforgiving servant (Matthew 18), and the shrewd manager (Luke 16).

Sometimes *a few of the details* of the parable will be used in the interpretation. In the parable of the tenants (Matthew 21), for example, the identification of the landowner as God, the tenants as the Jewish leaders, the servants as the prophets, and the son as Jesus—interpreting these details helps emphasize the one point the parable teaches. Jesus is showing the leaders of the Jews that by rejecting God's prophets and his Son they are bringing God's just judgment on themselves.

However, to identify the wall around the vineyard as the Mosaic law that separated Israel from the Gentiles, the winepress as Jerusalem where the people gathered to make sacrifices, the tower as the temple where God was present to watch over his chosen people, the fruits as the good works God expected of the people—interpreting these details would not support the real meaning of the parable. Instead, this would lead to developing many other lessons from the parable that are not really there. Parables of this type in which a few details are interpreted include the unfruitful fig tree (Luke 13), the talents (Matthew 25), and the ten minas (Luke 19).

In some parables almost all of the details are interpreted because they help teach the one intended truth of the parable. Matthew 13 has three such parables: the sower, the weeds, and the net.

Parables with an extension

Some parables have an obvious extension. The extension teaches a second spiritual truth, which usually is related to the truth of the first part of the parable.

In the parable of the prodigal son, Jesus pictures God's full and free forgiveness of the repentant sinner. In an extension that deals with the older son, Jesus shows us that God wants the Christian who has remained faithful to forgive and receive back the prodigal in the same way the heavenly Father does. Other parables of this type are the rich man and Lazarus (Luke 16), which has an extension about the rich man's brothers, and the parable of the wedding banquet (Matthew 22), with an extension involving the man without a wedding garment.

Characteristics of Jesus' parables

All of Jesus' parables involve true-to-life situations whether they involve people or plants or animals. They are not like Aesop's fables in which animals and plants talk. It would not have been wrong for Jesus to use those kinds of stories to teach a lesson. He just chose not to use them. In the Old Testament, on the other hand, Jotham used a parable in which trees and a vine and a thornbush talked when he rebuked the citizens of Shechem (Judges 9).

The fact that Jesus' parables are true to life does not mean, however, that every incident mentioned in a parable actually took place. We cannot ascertain, for example, whether the good Samaritan and poor Lazarus were actual people, or whether Jesus' parables about these men were stories he composed based on some true-to-life experiences of the poor or of people on the road to Jericho.

Jesus' parables can be classified as either direct (typical) or indirect (symbolic). In a direct parable, Jesus uses a human being as the known, and the spiritual lesson is demonstrated right in the life of that person. The good Samaritan is a neighbor to a person in need; the publican went home justified rather than the Pharisee; Lazarus was taken to heaven and the rich man ended up in hell.

In the indirect parables the incident described is purely physical. The spiritual lesson parallels what happens in the parable but does not take place in the parable itself. Some examples of indirect parables are the hidden treasure, the mustard seed, the yeast in the batch of dough, the fish net, and the wedding banquet.

Jesus also repeated some of his parables on a second occasion. Usually in his second use of a parable, he changed a few of the details because he wanted to teach a somewhat different lesson to a different group of people. When one remembers that Jesus taught publicly for several years, it is not surprising that this happened often. One example is the parable of the ten minas (Luke 19) and the parable of the talents (Matthew 25). They are similar in structure and content, but the occasion and the aim are different.

Jesus told essentially the same parable on different occasions to teach somewhat different lessons.

The same is true of the parables of the great banquet (Luke 14) and the wedding banquet (Matthew 22). In Matthew 22 Jesus pictures how God will abandon the chief priests and Pharisees for their rejection of God's invitation and how God will gather others to take their place at the heavenly banquet. In Luke 14 Jesus is replying to a person who is seated at a meal with him. The man suggests that it will truly be wonderful to feast in God's heavenly kingdom. Jesus' parable is a warning to people like this man that someday, because of their concern for everything but spiritual matters, they may find themselves on the outside looking in at the poor and down-trodden seated at God's banquet.

Though one point has been emphasized throughout this discussion of parables, it is so important that it needs to be repeated one more time. The interpretation of parables must be restricted to the one point of comparison. The interpreter needs to use constant and discriminating judgment in the interpretation of parables. There is little danger that he will underinterpret a parable, but he can easily fall into over-interpretation.

Figurative language: types and symbols

The Holy Spirit also led the writers of Scripture to use types and symbols. Emphasis needs to be laid on the words "the Holy Spirit led." This is true because, as with all figurative language used in the Bible, some interpreters down through the ages have been tempted to let their imagination run wild in dealing with these two figures of speech.

In using types and symbols, the inspired writers, led by the Holy Spirit, are saying that a given item has an additional thought lying behind it in addition to what one sees on the surface. No one has the right to subjectively add anything to what Scripture says, and so, no one has the authority to declare something a type or symbol unless the Holy Spirit led a biblical writer to clearly label it as such.[11]

A *symbol* does not teach a person something. Rather, it is an item that is used to remind one of something he already knows. One of the most familiar symbols we wear or place in prominent places in our homes and churches is the cross. This symbol reminds us of the price our Savior paid to redeem us. A cross will not teach anything to a person who knows nothing about Christ. But to us who know him, it serves as a simple yet vivid reminder of his saving work on our behalf.

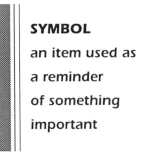

SYMBOL

an item used as

a reminder

of something

important

Perhaps the best known symbol God has given to the world is the rainbow. To those who do not know its origin, it is nothing more than a beautiful phenomenon during or after a rain. Whenever a believer sees it, he is reminded of God's promise never again to destroy the world by a flood (Genesis 9:12-16).

A *type* is a picture or pattern of something that lies in the future. Types in the Old Testament pictured something about Christ for the people who lived before Christ came. Types took the form of a person (Moses-Deuteronomy 18:15), a place (the Most Holy Place— Hebrews 9:3,8,12,25), an office (High Priest—Psalm 110:4 and Hebrews 9:6,7,11,12), a festival

TYPE

a person, item,

or event that is

a picture

of something

that lies

in the future

such as the Sabbath (Colossians 2:16) or the Day of Atonement (Hebrews 9:25,26), or an event (Israel called out of Egypt—Matthew 2:15). Most of the Old Testament types, like most of the Old Testament prophecies, pointed especially to Christ's saving work.

In working with types, the interpreter will note the one point of comparison between the type and its fulfillment (the antitype). This will help him determine in what respect the former prefigures or represents the latter. For example, the writer to the Hebrews speaks of the Most Holy Place as a type (Hebrews 9). It would be wrong to try to find an antitype for everything that was found in the Old Testament Most Holy Place such as the golden jar of manna, Aaron's rod which budded, and the stone tablets.

As in the interpretation of parables and other shorter figures of speech which were discussed earlier, there is only one proper procedure. Identify the one point of comparison, explain it, and interpret only those details which help explain the one point of comparison between the type and the antitype.

The fact that there are some types in Scripture does not give the interpreter the license to designate an item as a type simply because he sees a similarity between something in the Old Testament and something about Christ.[12] For example, it is easy to imagine that Isaac at Mount Moriah serves as a type of Christ. He was Abraham's only and beloved son. He carried the wood up the mountain and was willing to submit to death as a sacrifice. The only type in this passage, however, is the ram that became the substitute sacrifice.

The real point of Abraham's sacrifice of Isaac is God's test of Abraham's faith. This is evident from the introductory words to the account in Genesis 22:1 and from the words of the angel of the Lord to Abraham in Genesis 22:15-18. The writer to the Hebrews confirms this when he refers to this incident as God's test of Abraham's faith, not as a type (Hebrews 11:17).

If a person uses a text such as this as a type in his preaching or teaching, it would not necessarily mean that he is guilty of false doctrine. But it would mean that he is preaching something he imagined, not what he gleaned from the text as the result of proper interpretation. Furthermore, introducing a type which is not indicated by the Holy Spirit usually leads to an interpretation which either completely loses sight of the real purpose of the passage or puts the main point of the passage into the background.[13]

How one can go far afield in the matter of types once he lets his imagination loose is illustrated by W. Graham Scroggie's exposition of the life of Joseph.[14] Someone might protest that the following example is carrying the development of types too far. But anyone who uses his imagination to create types that the Holy Spirit has not indicated has forfeited his right to protest since he has crossed the same line as Scroggie.

Scroggie has Joseph serving as a type of Jesus in no less than 17 different ways:

1. He was the beloved son.
2. He was hated by his brothers.
3. His kingship was rejected.
4. He was conspired against.
5. He was stripped.
6. He was sold for silver.
7. He went into and came out of Egypt.
8. Two others were bound with him (one of whom was saved, the other lost).
9. He was righteous in his conduct.
10. He was released by the king.
11. He had great wisdom.
12. All power was given to him.
13. He served all nations.
14. He was not known by his brothers.
15. He was made known through an interpreter.
16. He was a fruitful bough.
17. All that happened was directed by God.

One might suggest, if one were to let his imagination loose for a moment, that Scroggie overlooked two of the best ways that Joseph is similar to Christ:

1. He had no thought of anger or revenge.
2. He was accused and suffered for a crime of which he was not guilty.

101

Imagining an implied sense for the words of Scripture is always illegitimate interpretation. It makes no difference whether it is narrative or apocalypse, simile or metaphor, allegory or parable, symbol or type. No matter how sanctified we might think our imagination is, we need to remember that subjectivity has no place in the interpretation of God's inspired Word.

Chiasm

Earlier in this chapter the importance of taking into account the genre of a passage was emphasized. In that connection the literary technique of parallelism in Hebrew poetry was mentioned. But parallelism is not limited to Hebrew poetry.

It seems that their Hebrew background led many of the biblical writers to include parallelism, sometimes very elaborate parallelism, in passages that could be designated as narrative or prophecy-teaching as far as their genre is concerned. Thus passages that include chiasm are found throughout Scripture. In the Old Testament they occur not only in the poetical books but also in the books of Moses as well as many prophetic books. As the examples that follow will show, chiasms occur in the gospels. But in the New Testament, chiasm occurs most often in the epistles of Paul and in the book of Revelation.[15]

Chiasm is a term based on the Greek letter *chi,* which looks very much like the English letter *x*. Chiasm refers to a literary construction that is characterized by two things: inversion and balance. Some chiasms are very simple and others are very complex.

Mark 2:27 is an example of a simple chiasm: "The Sabbath (A) was made for man (B), not man (B) for the Sabbath (A)." The two parts of this chiasm (A and B) are inverted and balanced. It could be diagrammed in one of two ways:

Note how the elements in the first diagram form a *chi* like the English *x*. In the second diagram note how B and B' are inset to indicate that they are the inner members of this chiasm.

As a chiasm becomes more complex, it may have six or more members. John 1:1-18 is an example of a complex chiasm:

A In the beginning was the Word, and the Word was with God, and the Word was God. He was with God in the beginning. (1,2)

  B Through him all things were made; without him nothing was made that has been made. (3)

    C In him was life, and that life was the light of men. The light shines in the darkness, but the darkness has not understood it. (4,5)

      D There came a man who was sent from God; his name was John. He came as a witness to testify concerning that light, so that through him all men might believe. He himself was not the light; he came only as a witness to the light. (6-8)

        E The true light that gives light to every man was coming into the world. He was in the world, and though the world was made through him, the world did not recognize him. (9,10)

          F He came to that which was his own, but his own did not receive him. (11)

            G Yet to all who received him, to those who believed in his name, (12a)

          F' he gave the right to become children of God—children born not of natural descent, nor of human decision or a husband's will, but born of God. (12b,13)

        E' The Word became flesh and made his dwelling among us. We have seen his glory, the glory of the One and Only, who came from the Father, full of grace and truth. (14)

      D' John testifies concerning him. He cries out, saying, "This was he of whom I said, 'He who comes after me has surpassed me because he was before me.'" (15)

    C' From the fullness of his grace we have all received one blessing after another. (16)

  B' For the law was given through Moses; grace and truth came through Jesus Christ. (17)

A' No one has ever seen God, but God the One and Only, who is at the Father's side, has made him known. (18)

Note how the lines labeled B or C or D, etc., all have a parallel thought and are arranged in an inverted order. Seeing the thoughts in a chiastic arrangement such as this does not change or alter the thought at all. But it does give us a sense of the beauty of this passage and a deeper appreciation of the thoughts being expressed.

In a chiasm it is important to note one other feature. In a longer chiasm such as the one printed above from John 1, the center of the chiasm (in this case, line G) is the climax of the thought. It is the one thought above all the others that the speaker or author wants to stress. Often, as in this case, it is the thought on which all the others hinge or are hung. Note in this John passage that the climactic thought, the thought on which all the others hinge, is that people receive Jesus in faith and believe on his name.

Summary

In the Bible, God speaks in human language. Before the pages of Scripture can be understood theologically, they must be understood grammatically, that is, in terms of the common usage of the biblical languages.

The first step is the study of the meaning each word has in a given context. The second step is the syntax of the words—how they are arranged in a group and the meaning they take from the particular way in which they are grouped. The interpreter will understand the words literally unless some of them are clearly designated as being figurative.

The task of the interpreter, then, is to find the one divinely intended sense of each passage since the only meaning of the words of Scripture is the simple, plain meaning.

NOTES

1. A number of lexicons are available for the interpreter to use. The basic Greek New Testament lexicon to consult first is

Bauer-Arndt-Gingrich-Danker (*A Greek New Testament and Other Early Christian Literature*). The strength of this lexicon is that it not only gives word meanings, but it also indicates where the word is used with different shadings in the New Testament. In addition, as the title indicates, it gives citations from other early Christian literature. These citations are noted under the various shadings of meanings so that one has an indication not only where the word was used, but also how. Citations are also given from the Septuagint and the Old Testament apocrypha, from published collections of inscriptions, from papyri and other Greek writers, and from writings of antiquity such as Strabo, Herodotus, Aristophanes, Solon, Socrates, Plato, etc. Finally, references are included from Moulton and Milligan (*The Vocabulary of the Greek Testament*) whenever the latter has information on New Testament words taken from the papyri and other non-literary sources.

A second important source of information on word meanings is Gerhard Kittel's *Theological Dictionary of the New Testament*. This lexicon does not have every New Testament word. Instead, it takes selected words and studies them in greater depth than Bauer-Arndt-Gingrich-Danker. Kittel will trace the use of a word beginning in the Greek world, then in the Septuagint and Judaism in general, and finally in the New Testament. There are nine volumes with a tenth volume as an index. The ten-volume set also has been abridged into one volume. Because Kittel traces the history of the use of a word, it is often very helpful to the interpreter in working with some of the key words in the New Testament. Some of the writers of articles on individual words reflect a historical-critical bias in their articles. In using Kittel, therefore, one may have to discount some of what is said, especially in regard to a word's use in the New Testament.

A third valuable lexicon is Louw and Nida's *Greek-English Lexicon of the New Testament Based on Semantic Domains*. As the title suggests, this lexicon differs from the others in that it lists words by semantic domains rather than alphabetically. In other words, instead of having all the shadings of meanings of a word listed in one place, the word is listed a number of times wherever each of its shadings fits together with words that are synonyms. The advantage for the interpreter in this arrangement is that he sees a particular word alongside all of its synonyms. He is enabled, therefore, to consider what distinguishes this word in meaning from its synonyms. This, in turn, gives him a better insight into just what nuance of meaning the Holy Spirit wished to indicate by the use of this word in a particular context. To make the use of this lexicon a little easier, the index is contained in a separate volume.

Thayer's *Greek-English Lexicon of the New Testament* is an older lexicon that was published in the late 1880s. It does not have any of the information that has been learned from the papyri, but it does have some brief notes on synonyms, which are helpful. It has been reprinted in paperback and so can be purchased for a very reasonable price. The most complete treatment of synonyms can be found in Trench's *Synonyms of the New Testament.*

Another old standard which can prove valuable at times for New Testament study is Liddell and Scott's *A Greek-English Lexicon.* It gives an exhaustive treatment of words in classical Greek along with Septuagint and New Testament references.

The best Hebrew Old Testament lexicons are (1) Brown-Driver-Briggs' *A Hebrew and English Lexicon of the Old Testament* (a translation of Gesenius' German lexicon) and (2) Koehler-Baumgartner's *Lexicon in Veteris Testamenti Libros.* Both contain useful and detailed references to cognates in other Semitic languages. The former lacks the information from Ugaritic, the Qumran finds, and other linguistic finds, which the latter supplies. William Holladay's *A Concise Hebrew and Aramaic Lexicon of the Old Testament* is based on the second edition of Koehler-Baumgartner. It is more up-to-date and very reliable but does not contain the useful references to cognates in other Semitic languages found in the other two lexicons.

The vocabulary help provided on computer programs can be very useful because of the instant access it provides to the information contained in lexicons.

2. Perhaps the most helpful Greek concordance is Moulton and Geden's *A Concordance to the Greek Testament* (Edinburgh, T. & T. Clark, 1970). Another good Greek concordance is Schmoller's *Handkonkordanz* (Stuttgart: P. W. B., 1949).

An old standard which lists both Old Testament and New Testament words according to the English translation (keying particularly off the KJV) and then gives the Hebrew Old Testament or Greek New Testament word after each English word is Young's *Analytical Concordance to the Bible.* Another concordance similar to Young's but keying off a number of contemporary translations and giving English transliterations of the Greek words is Darton's *Modern Concordance to the New Testament* (Garden City, NY: Doubleday & Co., Inc., 1976). Some of the contemporary translations also have a concordance in English only, which can be of some help (e.g., *The NIV Complete Concordance* by Goodrich and Kohlenberger, Grand Rapids: Zondervan Publishing Corporation, 1981).

A standard Old Testament Hebrew concordance for quite a few years has been Mandelkern's *Veteris Testamenti Concordantiae Hebraicae atque Chaldaicae.* It is written in only Hebrew and Latin. Another useful concordance is one by G. Wigram, *The Englishman's Hebrew and Chaldee Concordance of the Old Testament.* It provides a list of different English words used to translate a Hebrew word, as well as the various Hebrew words translated by the same word in English.

3. The three New Testament grammars which stand out from the rest of the crowd are Robertson's *A Grammar of the Greek New Testament,* Blass-Debrunner-Funk's *A Greek Grammar of the New Testament,* and Moulton's *A Grammar of New Testament Greek* (Volume 3, by Nigel Turner). Robertson's grammar is written in narrative style. It is quite detailed, making it necessary at times to wade through a page or two before one finds the point he is seeking. Blass-Debrunner-Funk's grammar is easy to work with because everything is arranged in numbered paragraphs, but it does not have the detail of the other two. Moulton's grammar has a summary of a grammatical point in narrative form followed by more detail in fine print. The fine print supplies numerous cross references for the interpreter to study the use of a grammatical point in most, if not all, of the other Septuagint, New Testament, and other koine uses. Moule's *An Idiom—Book of New Testament Greek* and Burton's *Syntax of Moods and Tenses in New Testament Greek,* as the titles suggest, give the interpreter valuable help with special problems in working with the Greek New Testament.

Old Testament Hebrew grammars include the *Gesenius Hebrew Grammar* translated by A. Cowley and *Hebrew Syntax—An Outline* by R. William.

A computer program developed by Gramcord Institute (Vancouver, WA) offers unparalleled syntactical and grammatical research capabilities including instant parsing and full statistical and graphical analysis. It is available for both IBM and Macintosh computers.

4. A good example is Robertson's treatment of *eis aphesin* ("for the forgiveness of sins") in Mark 1:4 and Acts 2:38. Robertson says that *eis* with the accusative expresses aim or purpose (p. 594). But then he says that this is not necessarily the case in these two passages. Though he grants that purpose is the meaning "in the abstract," he insists that, "It remains a matter for the interpreter to decide" (p. 595). In another place (p. 389), he also says about this construction that this is one time when the theologian has to step in before the grammarian is through.

Why does he make such an exception? Because if he were to let the Greek syntax stand, his Reformed belief that Baptism is not a means of grace would receive a severe blow. His theological bias will not allow the Greek to say what it does, namely, that people were baptized for the purpose of having their sins forgiven.

5. Luke 7:47 is a good example. Jesus says of the woman, "Her many sins have been forgiven—for she loved much." The Greek conjunction *hoti* ("for") can either be causal or evidential. The idea of cause, though a syntactical possibility, would contradict all that Scripture says elsewhere about the forgiveness of sins. God does not forgive anyone as a reward—the woman did not earn forgiveness because of the great love she had shown to Jesus. The evidential sense of "for," the other syntactical possibility, is the proper interpretation because it is the only interpretation that agrees with what Scripture says about forgiveness and love. Our love of Jesus is the result of forgiveness, not its cause. Thus love is also the evidence that we have been forgiven. It is our natural response to the great mercy that God gives us as a free gift for Jesus' sake.

That the latter is the meaning of this passage is made clear from several items in the context: (1) The story Jesus told to

Simon speaks of love as the natural response to having a large debt forgiven, not the cause or the reason why one is forgiven (v. 42); (2) Jesus' words which follow in verse 47 cite a lack of love as evidence of one who has been forgiven little; and (3) Jesus' clear words in verse 50 show that the woman's faith is what saved her.

So what Jesus says in verse 47 is that this woman's great love for Jesus was evidence of her understanding that her great burden of sin was forgiven through Jesus her Savior. Simon's lack of love, on the other hand, was evidence of his self-righteous attitude, which led him to feel very little need for forgiveness.

6. In 1 Thessalonians 4:4, for example, the words *skeuos ktasthai* are interpreted as meaning either controlling the body or acquiring a spouse. Although both meanings fit the context, which is speaking of sexual sins, two things point to the latter of the two as the better interpretation: (1) The present tense of the verb *ktasthai* favors the meaning "acquire"; and (2) In verse 6 Paul warns against wrongdoing or taking advantage of a brother "in this matter," referring back to verse 4. The meaning of acquiring a spouse fits better with the thought of not taking advantage of a brother than the meaning of controlling the body does. Still, this understanding has one weakness, namely, understanding *skeuos* to mean a spouse. So though one may favor the interpretation of acquiring a spouse, it is impossible to insist that the other understanding is wrong.

7. When two Christians cannot agree on which of the two interpretations (both of which are allowable according to syntax and not in conflict with any other portion of Scripture) fits the context best, the matter under discussion is called an "exegetical question." This expression does not refer to an agreement to differ in doctrine but only to allowing the two (on rare occasions, the three) differing scriptural explanations to stand as possible interpretations of the passage in question.

8. Jesus' words in Mark 4:11,12 are sometimes explained in this way. These words do not say that Jesus spoke in parables so that his disciples would understand and so that those on the outside would not understand. Note the quote Jesus uses from Isaiah (in verse 12) to explain what he means.

This quote does not say that God was hiding things from the hearers. Rather, Isaiah was to proclaim God's message to the people so plainly that they could not misunderstand. But because the people did not want to hear what God said, the more clearly they understood what Isaiah said, the more they would harden themselves against it. They would "see" and "hear," and the only reason they would not "perceive" and "understand" would be that they chose not to.

Note the parallel account in Matthew 13 where Jesus says that his parables would have the effect of taking away from unbelieving people what little they had (Matthew 13:12). This would happen not because they couldn't understand. Rather, it would happen because their hearts became calloused and they closed their eyes just as the people at Isaiah's time did (Matthew 13:15). Matthew also emphasizes that it was particularly in this way that Jesus fulfilled the prophet's words, which said that the Messiah would reveal things to the people that were hidden since the creation of the world (Matthew 13:34,35).

Likewise, Mark in a summary statement emphasizes that in Jesus' constant use of parables he spoke only "as much as they could understand" (Mark 4:33). The objection is sometimes raised that Jesus' own disciples did not always understand and so Jesus had to explain parables such as the sower and the seeds to them. But Jesus did not do so without rebuking his disciples for their failure to understand. In fact, their failure to understand this particular parable led Jesus to wonder how they would ever understand any parable (Mark 4:13).

9. Scripture's use of "sleep" to refer to death should not be understood as a euphemism. Sleep is not used to avoid the mention of death. Instead it is a metaphor to picture what death is really like for believers. It is not the end for them, but it is like a sleep from which Jesus will someday awaken them to life everlasting. Jesus used this metaphor of sleep for death in the home of Jairus (Mark 5:39). He also used it in regard to Lazarus to indicate to his disciples that for him to raise Lazarus from the dead was the same as waking a person from sleep (John 11:11-15). Paul used this metaphor to comfort the Thessalonians about their loved ones who had died in faith (1 Thessalonians 4:13,14), and urged them to use it in comforting one another (4:18).

10. The words Paul uses in Galatians 4:24 are *atina estin alle-goroumena*. A literal translation of these words would be, "Which things [i.e., the two wives and the two sons] are being allegorized [a present, passive verb with Paul as the implied agent]." In other words, in verses 24-27 the wives are used to represent the two covenants, and in verses 28-31 the resolution of the problem involving the two sons is used to illustrate what needs to be done in Galatia.

11. Note the emphasis of the writer to the Hebrews in speaking of the Old Testament tabernacle and the ceremonies which took place there as types of Christ. "The Holy Spirit was showing by this . . ." (Hebrews 9:8).

12. Care must be taken to distinguish between a type and an analogy. A type pictures something which lies in the future while an analogy often reaches back into the past to picture something. For example, Jesus' comparison of his death on the cross to the brass serpent Moses put up on the pole in the wilderness is an analogy and not a type. It is not said or even implied in the Old Testament account that the people who looked at the brass serpent thought of it as a type of Christ. Rather, Jesus is simply using an analogy by which he reaches back to an Old Testament event to help Nicodemus understand how all who believe God's promise connected with the uplifted Savior will be saved by faith (John 3:14-21).

13. The writer of this book on interpretation once preached on Isaac at Mount Moriah as a type of Christ in a sermon suggested by Golladay's *Lenten Outlines and Sermons* (Columbus: Lutheran Book Concern, 1935). An elderly lady who had a good Bible understanding had some very complimentary words for the sermon as she left church that evening. She commented, "That sermon was very informative. I have read that chapter many times, but I never realized that Isaac was a picture of Christ." Though her words were sincerely complimentary, they awakened in the preacher a realization that his sermon that evening had been more imagination than interpretation.

14. W. Graham Scroggie, *The Unfolding Drama of Redemption* (Grand Rapids: Zondervan Publishing Corporation, 1970), p. 129.

15. For a complete treatment of chiasms see Nils Lund's *Chiasmus in the New Testament* (Peabody, MA: Hendrickson Publishers, Inc., 1992).

BIBLIOGRAPHY—CHAPTER SIX

Black, D. A. *Linguistics for Students of New Testament Greek.* Grand Rapids: Baker Book House, 1988.

Franzmann, M. "Essays in Hermeneutics." *Concordia Theological Monthly,* August to October, 1948.

————. "The Art of Exegesis." Compendium Concordia Cassette Program. St. Louis: Concordia Publishing House, 1972.

Fuerbringer, L. *Theological Hermeneutics.* St. Louis: Concordia Publishing House, 1924.

Mickelsen, A. B. *Interpreting the Bible,* Chapters 6,8-15. Grand Rapids: William B. Eerdmans Publishing Co., 1972.

Kaiser, W., and M. Silva. *An Introduction to Biblical Hermeneutics,* Part 2. Grand Rapids: Zondervan Publishing Corporation, 1994.

Kearly, Myers, and Hadley (eds.). *Biblical Interpretation: Principles and Practices.* Grand Rapids: Baker Book House, 1986.

Surburg, Raymond. *Principles of Biblical Interpretation.* Chapters 7,9,10,15-26,29. Fort Wayne: Concordia Theological Seminary Press, 1984.

Zuck, R. B. *Basic Bible Interpretation,* Chapters 5-9. Wheaton, IL: Scripture Press, 1991.

7

THE ONLY SAFE AND TRUE INTERPRETER OF SCRIPTURE IS SCRIPTURE ITSELF: THE SCRIPTURAL SETTING

Historical-grammatical-scriptural interpretation

As the two previous chapters have shown, proper interpretation gives both the historical and grammatical settings their due. There are many Christians who have espoused and defended the historical-grammatical method and resisted the inroads of the modern tool of Satan, the historical-critical method (see Part Three). The question remains: What sets Lutheran interpretation apart from the others who practice the historical-grammatical method of interpretation?

In Roman Catholicism, the final arbiter of what a passage means is what the church says it means. Yes, the historical and grammatical settings are carefully considered by conservative Catholics. But when the final decision about meaning is made, the interpreter must make sure that his conclusions agree with the tradition of the church as it has been set forth by the bishops in council and by the pope.[1]

Scripture does urge us to remember the leaders in the church who have gone before us and to imitate their faith

(Hebrews 13:7). But Scripture also warns us to beware of leaders in the church who are Satan's agents to introduce false doctrine and try to lead God's people away from the truth:

> Matthew 24:24 For false Christs and false prophets will appear and perform great signs and miracles to deceive even the elect—if that were possible.

> Acts 20:29,30 I know that after I leave, savage wolves will come in among you and will not spare the flock. Even from your own number men will arise and distort the truth in order to draw away disciples after them.

> 2 Peter 2:1 There will be false teachers among you. They will secretly introduce destructive heresies, even denying the sovereign Lord who bought them—bringing swift destruction on themselves.

> 1 John 2:18 Dear children, this is the last hour; and as you have heard that the antichrist is coming, even now many antichrists have come. This is how we know it is the last hour.

A special warning is also given about the Antichrist (fulfilled in the papacy, 2 Thessalonians 2:3-12) who claims for himself the authority in the church to be the final judge of what God says or does not say. The Roman Catholic way of interpretation is not a proper way even though the historical-grammatical approach is used.

But don't Lutherans let Luther decide the meaning of a passage for them? No, true Lutherans do not use Luther as a pope. Instead, they imitate Luther in how they go about the interpretation of Scripture.

Among those of the conservative Reformed persuasion the final arbiter of what a passage means is reason. Yes, the historical and grammatical settings of passages are given great attention, and the context of Scripture is also considered. But in such important doctrines as conversion, election, the means of grace, and Christ's person and work, the meaning of a passage may be set aside or slightly altered because they believe the "power of reasoning" must finally "determine what the message means."[2]

But don't Lutherans let the Lutheran Confessions interpret Scripture for them? No, true Lutherans do not let anything but the inspired Scriptures serve as the final judge of what God says or does not say. We subscribe to the Lutheran Confessions because, in every subject they address, they are a true exposition of Scripture. But it would be a mistake on our part in determining a doctrinal matter if we would insist that we must make the Scriptures fit in with what we perceive the confessions to be saying.

What set Luther apart from other interpreters was his insistence that the only way an interpreter can be sure his interpretation is the correct one is if he lets Scripture itself determine for him what any given passage means. This does not happen by some kind of immediate illumination from God, but from the careful study of Scripture in which reason plays its proper role as servant, not master. In Luther's approach, besides considering the historical and grammatical settings, a third setting was all-important, namely, the scriptural setting.

Scripture must interpret Scripture, Luther insisted. The meaning of a given passage is determined only (1) by comparing what it says with all the other passages of Scripture which address the same subject in the same or similar words; and then (2) by letting what God said in all those other passages explain what God means by the words in the passage under  study. This is the only proper way to interpret a passage of Scripture because it is only in this way that God himself becomes the arbiter of what he means by those words.

SCRIPTURE interprets SCRIPTURE

How the interpreter puts Luther's approach into practice is the focus of this final chapter of Part One. The interpreter must be sure that at all times he is carrying out the Lord's admonition: "If a person speaks, let him say what God says" (1 Peter 4:11 GWN-NT, 1st ed.).

A third important adjective needs to be added if one's interpretation is to meet this standard. The method he uses must not only be the historical-grammatical method. It must be the historical-grammatical-scriptural method.

The unity of Scripture

The historical-grammatical-scriptural method of interpretation is based on the conviction that Scripture forms a perfect unity. The believer has learned to know by faith that there are no irreconcilable contradictions in Scripture. The presuppositions of faith (see chapter 1) assure those whom God has quickened and enlightened that the Bible forms a perfect unity in which there is no error or contradiction. Since God the Holy Spirit guided the writers of Scripture in every word they wrote, and since God can neither lie nor err, the believer knows that God's Word has a perfect unity.[3]

This unity is above all else a unity in doctrine because God's primary purpose in giving us his Word is to teach us the way of salvation. The Old Testament does not teach a God or a way of salvation that differs in any way from what the New Testament teaches. Paul does not teach a slant on justification that differs from what Jesus taught. John's writings do not teach a view of Christianity that contradicts Peter or James at times.

There are differences between the Old and New Testaments, between the gospels and the epistles, and between individual writers. But these differences are not contradictions. They are all relative differences, not absolute differences.

The following are several examples of what is meant by this. The Old Testament differs from the New in that it is a shadow of things to come while the New Testament presents the reality (Colossians 2:17). In speaking of justification, Paul differs from James because he is addressing those who want to add works to faith as the cause of justification while James is addressing those whose understanding of faith is that it is a purely intellectual matter, not a living and active faith. The gospels tell us of the life and death of God's Son by which he finished our redemption. The epistles spell out what Jesus' redemption means in greater detail, defend it against false teaching, and guide the children of God to respond to their redemption in faith-born love and fervent hope.

Because the differences, such as these, between various parts of the Bible are relative and not absolute, Scripture is a perfect unity. Peter's thoughts in his two epistles underscore why this is true.

He emphasizes that the words spoken by the prophets of the Old Testament and the apostles of the New Testament (2 Peter 3:2) are all from God (2 Peter 1:20,21).

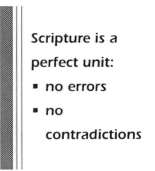

Scripture is a perfect unit:

- **no errors**

- **no contradictions**

> 2 Peter 3:2 I want you to recall the words spoken in the past by the *holy prophets* and *the command given by our Lord and Savior through your apostles.*

> 2 Peter 1:20,21 Above all, you must understand that no prophecy of Scripture came about *by the prophet's own interpretation.* For prophecy never had its origin in the will of man, but *men spoke from God as they were carried along by the Holy Spirit.*

Peter adds that the same Lord who guided the writers of the Old Testament to tell of God's coming salvation (1 Peter 1:10-12) also led men to record the eyewitness accounts of Jesus' life (2 Peter 1:16-18).

> 1 Peter 1:10-12 Concerning this salvation, the prophets, who *spoke of the grace that was to come to you,* searched intently and with the greatest care, trying to find out the time and circumstances to which the Spirit of Christ in them was pointing when he *predicted the sufferings of Christ and the glories that would follow.* It was revealed to them that they were not serving themselves but you, when they spoke of the things that have now been told you by those who have preached the gospel to you by the Holy Spirit sent from heaven. Even angels long to look into these things.

> 2 Peter 1:16-18 We did *not* follow *cleverly invented stories* when we told you about the power and coming of our Lord Jesus Christ, *but we were eyewitnesses* of his majesty. For he received honor and glory from God the Father when the voice came to him from the Majestic Glory, saying, "This is my Son, whom I love; with him I

am well pleased." *We ourselves heard this voice* that came from heaven when we were with him on the sacred mountain.

Peter also speaks of those who wrote letters to specific groups of people in widely varying settings (1 Peter 1:1; 2 Peter 3:15).

> 1 Peter 1:1 Peter, an apostle of Jesus Christ, to God's elect, strangers in the world, *scattered throughout Pontus, Galatia, Cappadocia, Asia and Bithynia.*

> 2 Peter 3:15 Bear in mind that our Lord's patience means salvation, just as our dear brother *Paul also wrote you* with the wisdom that God gave him.

Finally, Peter says that these letters were written to instruct, warn, comfort, and encourage Christians (1 Peter 5:12; 2 Peter 1:12; 2 Peter 3:1,2; 2 Peter 3:17,18).

> 1 Peter 5:12 With the help of Silas, whom I regard as a faithful brother, *I have written to you briefly,* encouraging you and testifying that this is the true grace of God. Stand fast in it.

> 2 Peter 1:12 So *I will always remind you of these things,* even though you know them and are firmly established in the truth you now have.

> 2 Peter 3:1,2 Dear friends, this is now my second letter to you. I have written both of them *as reminders to stimulate you to wholesome thinking.* I want you to recall the words spoken in the past by the holy prophets and the command given by our Lord and Savior through your apostles.

> 2 Peter 3:17,18 Therefore, dear friends, since you already know this, *be on your guard* so that you may not be carried away by the error of lawless men and fall from your secure position. But *grow in the grace and knowledge* of our Lord and Savior Jesus Christ. To him be glory both now and forever!

The believer sees the perfect unity of the Bible in evidence on every page of Scripture. For him it is not only a constant assurance as he reads God's Word, but it is also a key factor in his interpretation of each verse.

Old Testament quotations in the New Testament

The use of quotations from the Old Testament in the New are important to the interpreter for two reasons. They clearly illustrate the unity of Scripture. They also underscore the fact that the inspired writers used Scripture to interpret Scripture.

The New Testament writers quote the Old Testament for a number of reasons. Some cite the Old Testament to show how an Old Testament prophecy was fulfilled. Matthew's gospel has many such quotations, which are introduced with the familiar words, "Then what was spoken by the prophet was fulfilled." In this way the close tie between the testaments is clearly established by stressing that the New Testament is the *fulfillment* of the Old.

OT QUOTES

- **fulfillment**
- **proof**
- **illustrative**

Sometimes the New Testament writers use Old Testament quotes as *proof passages*. In Romans 3:10-19, Paul quotes several passages from the psalms to prove the point he has made in chapters 1 and 2 "that Jews and Gentiles alike are all under sin" (3:9). The fact that the inspired writers used Old Testament passages as proof passages shows that they recognized a perfect unity between what the Old Testament prophets had written and what they themselves were saying.

Quite a number of Old Testament quotations are *illustrative*. Paul in particular uses this type of Old Testament reference frequently. In Romans 4:6 Paul quotes David's words as an example of the fact that God credits righteousness apart from works. In 1 Corinthians 10:7 Paul cites Exodus 32:6 as an illustration of the kind of evil he was warning them about. Jesus also used illustrative Old Testament passages to show the leaders of the Jews their sin in the way they handled Scripture (Matthew 15:3-9) and by their rejecting him (Matthew 21:42).

This use of Old Testament quotes underscores the unity of the Bible and also shows how God's Word in one part of Scripture can be used to explain or clarify another portion.

Some people draw some false conclusions from the fact that the Old Testament quotations are not always verbatim. They suggest that this may indicate the little regard that the New Testament writers had for the Old. They say, for example, that Paul's inexact quotes show a carelessness on his part, or that he quoted from a faulty memory because it was too bothersome for him to look up the passage in the cumbersome scrolls.

Peter shows that such a conclusion is not proper. Peter, who had such a high regard for every inspired word of the Old Testament (2 Peter 2:19-21), commended Paul's letters in their entirety as written "with the wisdom that God gave him (2 Peter 3:15,16). Why wasn't Peter bothered by the fact that Paul did not quote verbatim from the Old Testament? Simply because Peter knew that the same Holy Spirit who had inspired the Old Testament writers had also inspired Paul.

Peter also knew that Paul was free to quote from the Old Testament in a number of ways as long as the quote retained the basic substance of the Old Testament passage. Think, for example, of how our newspapers and magazines quote people. They may quote verbatim, or by paraphrasing, or in a general way. There is nothing wrong with this as long as they represent the substance of the original statement accurately. The same is true of Paul and all the other New Testament writers who quote the Old Testament.

The NT writers often quoted the substance of OT passages instead of quoting them verbatim.

The Holy Spirit guided New Testament writers to quote Old Testament passages in a number of ways in addition to quoting them verbatim.

1. The Holy Spirit guided New Testament writers to *refer to the content of an Old Testament passage in a general way*. In Ephesians 4:8 Paul changes Psalm 68:18 ("gave gifts" instead of "received gifts"). At first it might seem that he changed the substance of the verse, but upon examining the content of the psalm, one notes that the psalmist is talking about God going forth to destroy his people's enemies. God takes plunder from them (vv. 1,2,12-18,28-31) and then from his own bounty blesses

his people with many gifts (the rest of the psalm). So when Paul "quotes" this verse he is referring to the general content of the psalm and representing its substance faithfully even though he changes a key word.

2. The Holy Spirit guided New Testament writers *to paraphrase* an Old Testament passage. In Hebrews 10:37,38, the writer paraphrases Habakkuk 2:3,4 where God gives a revelation that he will not fulfill for quite some time. Habakkuk is told by God to tell the people that those who cling to God's promise in faith will be righteous. On the other hand, those who will not wait (Habakkuk 2:3 "Though it linger, wait for it"), who shrink back and abandon their faith because of the coming bad times, will be lost. The writer to the Hebrews is often misrepresented as changing the substance of Habakkuk somewhat. But if one realizes he is paraphrasing and not quoting, the substance is exactly the same.

3. The Holy Spirit led New Testament writers to *quote the Hebrew in either a loose* (compare Ephesians 4:8 and Psalm 68:18) *or a literal* (compare Matthew 2:15 and Hosea 11:1) *translation.*

4. The Holy Spirit led New Testament writers to *quote the Septuagint* Greek translation of the Old Testament (or a slightly altered Septuagint) when it translates the substance of the thought of the Hebrew accurately (compare Romans 4:7,8 and Psalm 32:1,2; or Luke 3:6 and Isaiah 40:5).

It is also significant that the contemporaries of the New Testament writers did not take issue with the way these writers quoted the Old Testament. The leaders of the Jews attacked Jesus for many things, but they did not criticize him when he paraphrased an Old Testament passage instead of quoting it verbatim. The believers in the early congregations did not find fault when the New Testament writers used the Septuagint to quote the Old Testa-

The contemporaries of the NT writers never criticized any of the ways that the NT writers quoted the OT.

ment or when they referred to the content of a passage in a general way.

We shouldn't be troubled by this either. Just the opposite is true. The use of Old Testament quotations in the New Testament clearly demonstrates the unity of Scripture. We also see this in the consistent way that the New Testament writers maintained the substance of the Old Testament passages when they quoted them in some way other than verbatim.

Fulfillment of prophecy

The prophecies of Scripture that have been fulfilled, most of which are Old Testament prophecies fulfilled in the New, are important to the interpreter for several reasons: (1) They demonstrate the unity of Scripture; and (2) Since most of them deal with the person and work of Christ, they underscore the Christocentricity of Scripture.

Many of the Old Testament prophecies that are fulfilled in the New are clearly identified by the inspired writers. Matthew, for example, in writing apparently for a mostly Jewish audience often says, "This took place to fulfill what the Lord said through the prophet."

In instances where one cannot find a passage in which a prophecy is expressly said to be fulfilled, the interpreter should determine whether all the essential elements of the prophecy are there in the person or event under consideration. In such a case the interpreter is justified in identifying the Old and New Testament passages with each other, particularly if the context of the prophecy is Messianic, or if no other historical person or event fulfills all the elements of the prophecy (e.g., Psalm 22:1 and Matthew 27:46).

> Psalm 22:1 My God, my God, why have you forsaken me? Why are you so far from saving me, so far from the words of my groaning?

> Matthew 27:46 About the ninth hour Jesus cried out in a loud voice, "Eloi, Eloi, lama sabachthani?"—which means, "My God, my God, why have you forsaken me?"

Some Old Testament prophecies have only one fulfillment in the New Testament. These we call direct prophecies. Some examples are Isaiah 7:14 and Matthew 1:22,23; Psalm 16:9-11 and Acts 2:26-31.

> Isaiah 7:14 Therefore the Lord himself will give you a sign: The virgin will be with child and will give birth to a son, and will call him Immanuel.

> Matthew 1:22-23 All this took place to fulfill what the Lord had said through the prophet: "The virgin will be with child and will give birth to a son, and they will call him Immanuel"—which means, "God with us."

> Psalm 16:9-11 Therefore my heart is glad and my tongue rejoices; my body also will rest secure, because you will not abandon me to the grave, nor will you let your Holy One see decay. You have made known to me the path of life; you will fill me with joy in your presence, with eternal pleasures at your right hand.

> Acts 2:26-32 "Therefore my heart is glad and my tongue rejoices; my body also will live in hope, because you will not abandon me to the grave, nor will you let your Holy One see decay. You have made known to me the paths of life; you will fill me with joy in your presence." Brothers, I can tell you confidently that the patriarch David died and was buried, and his tomb is here to this day. But he was a prophet and knew that God had promised him on oath that he would place one of his descendants on his throne. Seeing what was ahead, he spoke of the resurrection of the Christ, that he was not abandoned to the grave, nor did his body see decay.

Other prophecies have a double fulfillment, one in the Old Testament and the ultimate fulfillment in the New. Two examples of double-fulfillment prophecies are Zechariah 11:12,13 and Matthew 27:9,10; 2 Samuel 7:11-16 and Luke 1:32,33.

> Zechariah 11:12,13 I told them, "If you think it best, give me my pay; but if not, keep it." So they paid me thirty pieces of silver. And the LORD said to me, "Throw it to the potter"—the handsome price at which they priced me! So I took the thirty pieces of silver and threw them into the house of the LORD to the potter.

Matthew 27:9,10 Then what was spoken by Jeremiah the prophet was fulfilled: "They took the thirty silver coins, the price set on him by the people of Israel, and they used them to buy the potter's field, as the Lord commanded me."

2 Samuel 7:11-16 The LORD declares to you that the LORD himself will establish a house for you: When your days are over and you rest with your fathers, I will raise up your offspring to succeed you, who will come from your own body, and I will establish his kingdom. He is the one who will build a house for my Name, and I will establish the throne of his kingdom forever. I will be his father, and he will be my son. When he does wrong, I will punish him with the rod of men, with floggings inflicted by men. But my love will never be taken away from him, as I took it away from Saul, whom I removed from before you. Your house and your kingdom will endure forever before me; your throne will be established forever.

Luke 1:32,33 He will be great and will be called the Son of the Most High. The Lord God will give him the throne of his father David, and he will reign over the house of Jacob forever; his kingdom will never end.

The importance of context

Since the Bible is a perfect unity, every part of the Bible must be interpreted in the light of the context, both the immediate and the wider context. Those who teach false doctrine often are guilty of taking a passage out of its immediate context or ignoring the wider context of all of Scripture.

CONTEXT

immediate

and

wider

As an example of lifting a passage out of its context and giving it a different meaning, Rudolph Bultmann likes to quote Luke 9:23-25 in support of his existentialist view of what it means to die and rise with Christ (see chapter 10). However, the preceding verse speaks of Jesus' death and resurrection as a real event, not as a "spiritual change" which took place in him. The verse that follows speaks of a real judgment when Jesus comes in glory at the end of the world, not an eschatological experience in the present moment. Bultmann's interpretation is not at all what the context allows.

No passage of Scripture can be plucked out of its immediate context and be made to mean something other than what it means in that setting. We recognize that this kind of interpretation would be illegitimate if it were done in any other literature. How much more, then, must the interpreter of Scripture avoid lifting any passage out of its context if he is really interested in the right understanding of God's words!

What is true about the immediate context is equally true of a passage or a portion of Scripture and its relationship to the wider context of the Bible. The wider context of a passage might be the chapter or several chapters, the book or letter, the Old or New Testament, or the whole Bible. God cannot contradict himself and thus become a liar.

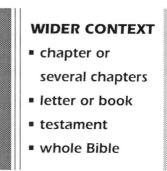

WIDER CONTEXT

- **chapter or several chapters**
- **letter or book**
- **testament**
- **whole Bible**

Titus 1:2 . . . a faith and knowledge resting on the hope of eternal life, which *God, who does not lie,* promised before the beginning of time.

Hebrews 6:18 God did this so that, by two unchangeable things *in which it is impossible for God to lie,* we who have fled to take hold of the hope offered to us may be greatly encouraged.

John 17:17 Sanctify them by the truth; *your word is truth.*

Since God is the author of all of Scripture, no passage can be understood in a way that would make it conflict with or contradict another passage or portion of Scripture.

Those who teach a millennium set up a doctrine that conflicts with the wider context of Scripture which teaches us:

1. Jesus' kingdom is not of this world (John 18:36).

2. When Jesus comes he will take us immediately to be with him forever in heaven (1 Thessalonians 4:16,17).

3. There is no second chance for those who died in unbelief (Hebrews 9:27; Matthew 25:1-13).

Passages that say that on Judgment Day God will judge believers according to their works dare not be isolated from what Scripture teaches about works being the fruit, and thus the proof of a living faith. These are but two examples among many that illustrate how vital it is for the Bible interpreter to study individual passages in the light of all the passages that clearly deal with a given subject.

The interpreter also needs to be very careful in deciding what to use as a "parallel passage." The parallel cannot just be a verbal parallel—that is, having the same words or phrases occur in both passages. A parallel passage must be a real parallel. It must clearly deal with the same subject matter. Not only must the same or similar words or phrases occur, but the same ideas, thoughts, or doctrines must be under discussion in both passages. Only when the passages correspond exactly in both words and substance can they be considered parallel passages.

> **PARALLEL PASSAGES** are only those passages that speak about the same thing in the same or similar words.

Figurative, difficult, and obscure passages

In working with passages that are figurative, difficult, or obscure, the unity of Scripture compels one to interpret the figurative in the light of the literal, the difficult in the light of the simple, and the obscure in the light of the clear. For example, a passage in which a doctrine is merely touched on with a passing reference must be interpreted in the light of those passages where the doctrine is taught in words that are clear and unmistakable.[4] In 1 Thessalonians 1:4 Paul merely mentions the fact of the Thessalonians' election, while in Ephesians 1:3-5 he explains what election means.

126

Everything said earlier about the immediate and wider contexts obviously applies here also. The only reason that figurative, difficult, and obscure passages are being discussed as a separate point is because their abuse has often been a ploy used by false teachers to mislead or deceive people. Those who search Scripture merely to confirm their own imaginations, "revelations," opinions, or prejudices will usually latch on to passages of this kind as a basis for their position.

Special care must be taken in the interpretation of figurative, difficult, or obscure passages.

Sometimes people object to the idea that a passage of Scripture could be difficult or obscure. However, Scripture itself tells us this is the case sometimes. Peter says (2 Peter 3:16) that some parts of Paul's letters contain "things that are hard to understand."

What is equally significant for the interpreter is Peter's statement in this same verse that such passages are the kind "which ignorant and unstable people distort, as they do the other Scriptures, to their own destruction." A statement of Scripture such as this should warn every interpreter to make sure he is always using the literal to interpret the figurative, the simple to explain the difficult, and the clear to throw light on the obscure.

Judgments and deductions

Using Scripture to interpret Scripture does not preclude making judgments and deductions that are clearly based on Scripture. In fact, such judgments and deductions are necessary for two basic reasons:

1. The Bible is not a book that supplies the church with formal doctrinal statements covering every truth that is taught in Scripture.

2. Scripture does not give us a code of rules that one can apply to every situation he may meet in life.

In the NT times believers must constantly make judgments and deductions based on the general principles God gives in his Word.

In the Old Testament God gave Israel laws that governed every aspect of their life—their worship, their food and drink, and their life as a nation. In the New Testament, however, God gives us only basic principles to guide us in making doctrinal or practical judgments and deductions. This does not mean that the doctrines are unclear or that we have no clear guide as to what God's will for our life is. It simply means that there will be times when the believer will have to consider a situation he faces in the light of the scriptural principles which apply and then prayerfully act according to his best judgment.

For example, when a person or a group of people with whom we are in fellowship becomes involved in false doctrine or practice, Scripture gives us two principles to apply:

1. Those faithful to the Word have *an obligation to warn* their brothers about their error more than once in order to try to rescue them from the spiritual havoc that their error portends (2 Corinthians 13:2; 2 Thessalonians 3:15; Titus 3:10; James 5:19,20; Jude 22,23).

2. If the warnings are ignored, or if the error is defended as the truth, those who are faithful have the *obligation to separate from the errorists* as a final act of warning to them (Romans 16:17; 2 Corinthians 13:2; Titus 3:10; 2 John 9-11).

Scripture gives us two clear principles. But Scripture does not give us a set of rules by which we can determine the precise hour or day when the warning is to stop and the separating is to begin. In each case we will have to make that judgment. To be faithful to both principles we will neither by haste violate the first principle nor allow sentiment to keep us from applying the second.

Another area in which Christians must constantly make judgments and decisions is the matter of adiaphora (things that God has neither commanded nor forbidden us to do). Many things are adiaphora for the New Testament Christian, but God has given us two broad principles to apply:

1. Everything not forbidden by God's Word is permissible, but not everything is beneficial and constructive (1 Corinthians 10:23); and

2. The Christian will not do what serves his own interest or preference, but in love he will do what serves the physical and spiritual good of others (1 Corinthians 10:24).

Obviously, in applying these two principles the Christian has many difficult yet necessary judgments and decisions to make.

Making judgments and decisions like these is not a denial of what has been said in this chapter about letting Scripture interpret Scripture. Rather, it is only by letting Scripture interpret Scripture that we can come to a good understanding of the principles involved so that we can apply them properly.

In order to make judgments and decisions that are based on the Scriptural principles, it will also be necessary that we grow up in all things into Christ (Ephesians 4:15) and make all our judgments as spiritual people who have the mind of Christ (2 Corinthians 2:15,16). Then our judgments and decisions will not be arbitrary but will always take careful note of each of the following guidelines set down by Dr. Adolph Hoenecke.[5] The judgments and deductions made by spiritual people and based on scriptural principles must:

1. Never confuse law and gospel.

2. Never violate the laws of logic.

3. Never contradict in the least any statement of Scripture.

4. Take their premises from Scripture.

5. Posit nothing that does not lie implicit in Scripture.

Principles and the applications of principles

In working with the principles God gives in Scripture, the interpreter needs to make one other important distinction. He must clearly distinguish between scriptural principles and the applications that Scripture makes of these principles. Unless one is careful, he could easily turn the application made by an inspired writer into a pseudo-principle. For example, the principle under discussion in 1 Corinthians 14:34,35 is not the silence of women in the church. The principle is "women must be in submission, as the Law says" (v. 34). Paul applies this principle in the Corinthian situation by instructing the women to be silent in those situations where speaking would violate the principle of submission (vv. 29-32).

The interpreter must be careful to clearly distinguish between universal principles and the application of scriptural principles.

On the other hand, the Bible interpreter may legitimately use an application of a principle to help clarify his understanding of that principle. God's words about the punishment for anyone who harms the fetus in the womb of a pregnant woman (Exodus 21:22-24) are part of the Mosaic law, and so the punishment prescribed is no longer binding in New Testament times. But when God makes this application of demanding the life of a person who destroys a life in the womb, it does make the principle clear that in God's sight the life in a womb is at all times a human life. Or take the example of Paul's application of the principle of regular giving when he told the Galatians and the Corinthians to lay aside a certain amount on the first day of every week (1 Corinthians 16:1,2). This application does not establish a principle that God demands everyone to make an offering of money every Sunday. But this application does give us one example of how we might put the principle of giving regular offerings into practice in our day.

In distinguishing between scriptural principles and their applications, we must distinguish first between what a universal principle is (i.e., a command of God that applies to all people for all time) and what an application of a principle is (i.e., a command of God given to a particular group of people at a particular time for a particular reason). The only proper way to make this distinction is to let Scripture interpret

Scripture as we consider each such passage in the light of its immediate context and also in the wider context of Scripture. There are three questions to consider[6] in determining whether a command in a given passage is a universal principle or merely an application of a scriptural principle:

1. Does the immediate context *limit who is addressed* by the statement or command? Paul's statement to Timothy about elders in 1 Timothy 5:17 is addressed to elders in general, so these words do not apply only to the elders in Ephesus with whom Timothy was working at the time. But Paul's statement to Timothy in 1 Timothy 1:3 about staying in Ephesus is addressed only to Timothy, so it applies only to him.

2. Does the statement or command have a *rationale* in the immediate context *that limits it in any way?* Paul tells the Corinthians (1 Corinthians 9:14) that those who hear the gospel should provide for those who preach the gospel to them. The multiple rationales he gives (the Lord has commanded this, four examples from everyday life, three examples from the law of Moses) make it abundantly clear that this is an obligation of all Christians, not just the Corinthians. On the other hand, the only rationale Paul gives for his command to set aside some money each Sunday is his desire to avoid the necessity of a hurried collection when he arrives in Corinth (1 Corinthians 16:2). This rationale makes it clear that this command applies only to the Corinthians.

3. Does the immediate or wider context of Scripture limit a statement or command *in regard to scope or time?* Paul's directive to the unmarried and the widows in 1 Corinthians 7:8 that they should remain unmarried is immediately qualified in verse 9 when Paul tells them to marry "if they cannot control themselves."

Using the preceding three questions will help us determine a number of important things, all of which have something to do with distinguishing scriptural principles from their applications:

1. Whether a statement or command of Scripture applies to all people of all time or to a limited number of people for a limited time.

2. Whether a command is given to all Christians (i.e., a command given to Christians because they are believers in Christ) or to a limited number of Christians (i.e., because they are Christians who live in a certain place and time or because of some other special circumstances in which these Christians find themselves.)

3. Whether a statement is a general principle or only an application of a principle.

Historical events often illustrate general truths, but they do not establish universal commands of God.

Sometimes interpreters try to establish general truths from historical events. Historical events often illustrate general truths but they cannot be used to establish them. For example, Abraham's concern to find a believing wife for Isaac and Samson's troubles after marrying an unbelieving wife are used to establish the rule that a Christian should marry only a believing spouse. These passages do illustrate the wisdom of finding a believing marriage partner, but they do not establish a command of God in regard to marriage.

Reason and faith

In the process of Bible interpretation, reason does have a role to play in working with the externals such as textual criticism, the historical setting, and the grammatical setting. But reason has "only a purely formal service to perform, namely to receive the thoughts of Scripture and to form clear concepts from them."[7] It is faith alone that enables us to understand and accept the truths of Scripture.

The interpreter must understand the proper relationship of faith and reason in Bible interpretation.

Since both reason and faith are involved in Bible interpretation, it is necessary to know their exact relationship in this process. Proper interpretation will never let man's reason take a superior position in working with the divine truths inerrantly revealed in Scripture and grasped by faith. Rather the interpreter will take his reason captive under the sum total of divinely revealed truth.

There are times when two doctrines that Scripture teaches seem to be contradictory according to human reason. For example, Scripture teaches that Jesus is true God and also true man in one person. Or consider the fact that Scripture teaches that the elect are saved entirely by God's doing, while others are lost entirely by their own doing. In instances such as these, we accept what Scripture teaches as the truth, while also acknowledging that we are not able to solve the mystery presented to our reason by these doctrines.

We know that God did not reveal mysteries such as these to confuse us. Rather, these doctrines are important for us to know because they are integral parts of his plan of salvation for us. They emphasize the marvelous grace that God has shown to us in Christ. Therefore, God's revelation of these mysteries also helps us grow in faith by leading us "to grasp how wide and long and high and deep is the love of Christ, and to know this love that surpasses knowledge" (Ephesians 3:18,19).

The key to letting reason and faith play their proper roles is to let Scripture interpret Scripture. This point has been repeated often in this chapter, but how exactly is this done? Perhaps it will help to summarize by indicating four basic steps for the interpreter to follow in the study of a given passage or portion of Scripture:

1. The interpreter lets his reason play its role in establishing the autograph if there are variants (chapter 4), in learning all he can about the background of the words (the historical setting, chapter 5), and in determining the meaning of the words themselves by a study of individual word meanings, syntax, and genre (the grammatical setting, chapter 6).

2. At each step of the way in number one, the interpreter brings the light of all of Scripture to bear on his conclu-

sions. He does this by moving in the hermeneutical circle from the phrase or clause to the sentence to the paragraph (the immediate context) to the chapter to the book to the testament to the whole of Scripture (the wider context) and then back to the verse again.

3. In the process of moving through the hermeneutical circle the interpreter will especially bear in mind three key considerations:[8]

- The difference between law and gospel
- The difference between the Old and New Testaments
- That Christ is the center of Scripture

4. If in the process of following the hermeneutical circle (#2) and bearing in mind the key considerations (#3) the interpreter finds anything in conflict with the conclusions his reason made (#1), he will reject that conclusion or alter it so it harmonizes with the rest of his study of that passage or portion of Scripture.

The only proper way of interpretation

As was noted earlier, the principle of interpreting everything in the total context of Scripture is a precious part of our Lutheran heritage. It was Luther's use of this principle that enabled him to stand firm in the knowledge that he was right even when he stood against most of the scholars of his day. The scholars could quote what the tradition of the church had been for centuries or what was more reasonable, but unless they could show Luther from the context of Scripture that his understanding of a passage was wrong, he stood firm.

It is the use of this principle that enables us to know that we too are right when we understand a passage in a way that others reject. If we have carefully studied all that God has to say in Scripture on the subject addressed in a given passage[9] in addition to all that the historical and grammatical settings contribute to the passage's meaning, then we have let Scripture interpret Scripture. We ought to stand firm in our understanding of that passage against any human arguments.

Like Luther, we should declare our willingness to give up that understanding only if it can be shown that we have misunderstood what God is saying in the immediate or wider biblical context or that we have erred in our use of the historical or grammatical setting. In this way we can demonstrate that neither sinful pride nor denominational influence is motivating our insistence that ours is the right understanding. Instead, we want to show that our motivation is the defense of the basic principle that God himself is the only safe and true interpreter of his Word. This is the only proper way of interpreting Scripture.

In summary, it is only as we focus on Christ and compare Scripture with Scripture that what the Bible says and what it means will be clarified for us and correctly explained by us. This is true simply because the only safe and true interpreter of Scripture is Scripture itself.

NOTES

1. The Second Vatican Council clearly reaffirmed for Catholics the interplay of Scripture, tradition, and the magisterium in the matter of revealed truth. (See *The Documents of Vatican II,* ed. by W. M. Abbott. New York: Association Press, 1966. pp. 107-110).

2. E. C. Fredrich, "Twentieth Century Reformed Thinking Analyzed and Evaluated," *Wisconsin Lutheran Quarterly,* Vol. 72, No. 1, p. 72.

   Consider also this quote from Erickson's *Christian Theology,* Vol. 1 (Grand Rapids: Baker Book House, 1983. p. 257): "A distinction must be drawn between legislative authority and judicial authority. In the federal government, the houses of Congress produce legislation, but the judiciary (ultimately the Supreme Court) decides what the legislation means. . . . This seems to be a good way to think of the relationship between Scripture and reason. Scripture is our supreme legislative authority. . . . *When we come to determine what the message means, however, and, at a later stage assess whether it is true, we must utilize the power of reasoning. . . .* While there is a dimension of the self-explanatory within Scripture, Scripture alone will not give us the meaning of Scripture." (emphasis added)

3. *This Steadfast Word* (a booklet of essays on the Holy Scriptures that were presented at the Lutheran Free Conference held at Waterloo, Iowa, in 1964, ed. by C. Lawrenz) underscores the importance of the unity of the Scriptures in almost all of the essays.

4. J. P. Koehler, *"Die Regeln der biblischen Hermeneutik,"* Wisconsin Lutheran Seminary Catalog, 1912-13, p. 22, 1-B-2.

5. A. Hoenecke, *Ev.-Luth. Dogmatik* (Milwaukee: Northwestern Publishing House, 1909), Vol. 1, pp. 333,334.

6. D. Kuske, "What in Scripture Is Universally Applicable and What Is Historically Conditioned?" *Wisconsin Lutheran Quarterly,* Vol. 91, No. 2, pp. 83-105.

7. J. P. Koehler, *op. cit.,* p. 20, I-A-3.

8. J. P. Koehler, *op. cit.,* pp. 26,27, III-A,B,C.

9. This is the way the study of dogmatics makes a major contribution to the proper interpretation of Scripture. In dogmatics, all the passages that deal with a given doctrine are studied in concert with one another. This kind of overall understanding is essential for the interpreter to let Scripture interpret Scripture. The organization of passages according to subject matter also assists the interpreter in locating and using all those passages that are truly parallel passages.

BIBLIOGRAPHY—CHAPTER SEVEN

Arndt, W. *Bible Difficulties & Seeming Contradictions.* St. Louis: Concordia Publishing House, reprint 1987.

Berkhof, L. *Principles of Biblical Interpretation.* Grand Rapids: Baker Book House, 1962.

Bohlmann, R. *Principles of Biblical Interpretation in the Lutheran Confessions.* St. Louis: Concordia Publishing House, 1968.

_____ . "Confessional Biblical Interpretation: Some Basic Principles." *Studies in Lutheran Hermeneutics.* Philadelphia: Fortress Press, 1979. pp. 189-213.

Franzmann, M. "Essays in Hermeneutics." *Concordia Theological Monthly,* August to October, 1948.

_____ . "The Art Of Exegesis." St. Louis: Concordia, 1972. Audio cassettes in the Compendium Concordia Cassette program.

Fuerbringer, L. *Theological Hermeneutics.* St. Louis: Concordia Publishing House, 1924.

Johnson, Elliott. *Expository Hermeneutics: An Introduction.* Grand Rapids: Zondervan Publishing Corporation, 1990.

Kaiser, W., Jr. *The Uses of the Old Testament in the New.* Chicago: Moody Press, 1985.

Lawrenz, C. J. (ed.). *This Steadfast Word.* Lutheran Free Conference Publications, 1965.

Lillegard, G. O. *Biblical Hermeneutics.* Unpublished seminary notes.

Linemann, E. *Is There A Synoptic Problem?* Grand Rapids: Baker Book House, 1992.

McKnight, Scot. *Introducing New Testament Interpretation.* Grand Rapids: Baker Book House, 1989.

Mickelsen, A. B. *Interpreting the Bible.* Grand Rapids: William B.Eerdmans Publishing Co., 1963.

Oswald, H., and G. Robbert. *Luther as Interpreter of Scripture.* St. Louis: Concordia Publishing House, 1982.

Rademacher, E. D., and R. D. Preus (eds.). *Hermeneutics, Inerrancy, & The Bible.* Grand Rapids: Zondervan Publishing Corporation, 1984.

Ramm, B. *Protestant Biblical Interpretation.* Boston: Wilde, 1957.

_____ . Hermeneutics. Grand Rapids: Baker Book House, 1972.

Surburg, R. F. *The Principles of Biblical Interpretation.* Chapters 6,8,12-14,27,28. Fort Wayne: Concordia Theological Seminary Press, 1984.

_____ . "Presuppositions of the Historical-Grammatical Method of Interpretation." *Springfielder,* March, 1975.

Zuck, R. B. *Basic Bible Interpretation.* Wheaton, IL: Victor Books, 1991.

Part Two

THE HISTORY
OF INTERPRETATION
FROM THE TIME OF CHRIST

8

FROM THE EARLY CHURCH
TO THE REFORMATION

It is interesting to see what has happened in the interpretation of the Bible since the time Christ lived on earth. The history of Bible interpretation is not a very happy story because Satan often succeeded in leading Christians away from the proper interpretation of the Bible in various ways over these twenty centuries.

We are not surprised that Satan would work hard at doing this. Whenever this enemy of God can get Christians to follow a false way of interpreting the Bible, obviously he is also making some progress in destroying the gospel by which God saves people. Looking at Satan's successes over the years warns us how important it is that we hold to the proper interpretation of the Bible so that we do not fall victim to his destructive wiles.

The early church—
allegorizing begins

The history of interpretation in the period from the early church to the Reformation can be summarized with one word: allegorizing.

ALLEGORIZING

SAYS = MEANS[1]

and MEANS[2]

and MEANS[3]

and MEANS[4]

Allegorizing means that in addition to the obvious meaning of words arranged in a sentence or paragraph, a second, third, and even a fourth meaning are given to those words.

Why would an interpreter do something like this? He would do it either because he is not willing to accept that what a writer or speaker says is what is really meant, or he may believe that what is said isn't all that is meant.

The trend toward allegorizing began in Alexandria in Egypt. After Alexander the Great founded this city in 332 B.C., it became a center for preserving and promoting Greek culture. At the same time, Alexandria was one of the great centers of scientific learning in the Roman Empire. If a person wanted to get a top-notch university education, Alexandria was definitely a place to go.

The combination of promoting Greek culture and emphasizing scientific learning led to a conflict that spawned allegorizing. In the Greek mythological writings, such as those of Homer, rain was explained as the result of Zeus' (the king of the Greek gods) emptying his washbowl on the earth after washing his hands. As the scientists at Alexandria began to understand that rain was a result of the natural processes of evaporation and condensation, Homer's explanation was clearly unacceptable.

How could this conflict be solved? Since Homer's writings had a deep hold on people in this city where Greek culture was so prevalent, the solution was to allegorize Homer's writings rather than to try to get rid of them. Homer's story about Zeus and rain was simply given a second, scientific, explanation.

The Jews who lived in Alexandria soon found that the Old Testament also placed them in conflict with the new wave of scientific learning. Events such as the fall into sin, the tower of Babel, God's choosing of Abraham and his descendants as a special people, Joseph in Egypt, Moses and the crossing of the Red Sea, Daniel in the lions' den, etc.—all these events are explained in the Bible in terms of divine cause and effect. That is, what happened was the direct result of God's guiding and directing things. The "scientific mind" that developed in Alexandria (not unlike some of the "scientific thought" of our day) tended to explain everything in terms of natural cause and effect. That is, everything happens on its own, not as the result of divine intervention.

Obviously there was a conflict between the Old Testament and scientific thought in Alexandria. In this setting, many Jews also began to use allegorizing to harmonize many events in the Old Testament not only with the scientific thought in Alexandria, but also with Greek culture. Aristobulus, for example, used allegorizing to say that Moses was really the originator of many of the thoughts in Greek philosophy and that the Greeks had really borrowed their ideas from him.[1] By doing this, the Jews in Alexandria might have evaded the conflict between the Old Testament and Greek culture and scientific thought, but they were not doing proper Old Testament interpretation.

Philo

Another example of a man who thought he was rendering a "service" to God by making the Old Testament correspond to contemporary thought in Alexandria was Philo. Philo lived at the same time as Christ. His "contribution" to allegorizing was to set down some guidelines about when allegorizing *must* be used to replace the literal meaning of a passage with an alternative meaning.

Sometimes Philo felt that the literal sense of a passage stated something that could be considered unworthy of God or that might imply a contradiction. Philo insisted that the interpreter should avoid any such embarrassment for God by finding a hidden meaning in the words of that passage. For example, when the Bible says that Adam "hid himself

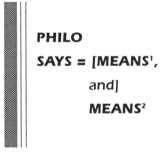

PHILO SAYS = [MEANS¹, and] MEANS²

from God," this dishonored God because God sees everything and no one can hide from him. Or when Abraham is called the "father" of Jacob, this implied a contradiction because Abraham was really Jacob's grandfather. It was this kind of thing, Philo said, for which the interpreter was obligated to find a different meaning.

Other passages that Philo said had to be allegorized were those with doubled expressions (e.g., "Abraham, Abraham"), superfluous words ("he led him forth outside"), repetition of facts, synonyms, a play on words, and anything abnormal in the grammar of a passage.[2] Hidden meanings were couched in such passages, he felt.

It is also worth noting that Philo would mention the literal meaning of such a passage only in passing as a sop to the weak and the ignorant. This kind of concession had to be made for the sake of those who did not have the sophisticated insights of the scholar in the study of Scripture. Philo was not the last Bible interpreter who, in accommodating himself to the "scientific" opinions of his day, displayed a condescending attitude toward the common layperson.

Down through history those who have used allegorizing have often belied the simple, plain meaning of the words of Scripture in order to make their peace with "scientific thought." This is also true of most of the historical-critical Bible interpreters of our day. As we shall see in chapter 10, their method is simply a contemporary form of Philo's allegorizing.

The allegorizing of the New Testament

Since allegorizing was firmly entrenched in Alexandria as the method of Old Testament interpretation, it is not surprising that when the New Testament came to Alexandria it was interpreted the same way. Most of the men who did this allegorizing wanted to prevent the New Testament from being ignored because of the devotion to science in this city. In their attempt to do this, they turned away from the literal meaning of the words of the New Testament. In the final analysis, what they did was a curse rather than a blessing for Bible interpretation. Over the centuries allegorizing became more and more subjective, resulting in fanciful interpretations and doctrinal errors.

Origen (A.D. 254) was one of the leaders of the early Christian church who encouraged the use of allegorizing to interpret the whole Bible. He suggested that every Bible passage ought to be given several meanings in order to match what he considered to be the threefold division of every human being: body, soul, and spirit. The three meanings he proposed for Bible interpretation were the literal sense (the body), the moral sense (the soul), and the mystical sense (the spirit).

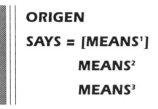

ORIGEN

SAYS = [MEANS[1]]

MEANS[2]

MEANS[3]

In order to find a meaning for a Bible passage that could be applied to the soul and the spirit, he had to allegorize. One example of his approach is the way he interpreted the event in which Rebecca came to draw water at the well and met Abraham's servant. Origen said that the "well" is Scripture and "Abraham's servant" is Christ. So the meaning of this passage in its mystical sense is that we must come to Scripture in order to meet Christ.[3] This isn't false doctrine, but it certainly isn't what Moses meant when he wrote those words.

This kind of allegorizing was vigorously opposed by the leaders of the church in Antioch in Syria. Chrysostom (A.D. 407) and Theodor of Mopsuestia (A.D. 428) upheld the literal sense of the words of Scripture against the allegorizing that was being done, especially in Alexandria. The church in Antioch condemned the idea that the historical events of the Bible had some additional, hidden meanings. The rules of grammar were upheld in Antioch as the way to arrive at the *objective* meaning of the words of Scripture and allegorizing was condemned as *subjective* imagination.

Jerome and Augustine

In spite of the opposition of some, such as those in the church at Antioch, allegorizing became commonplace. Two of the men who contributed to its extensive use were Jerome (A.D. 420) and Augustine (A.D. 430). Although they both used allegorizing, they also recognized the dangers involved in interpreting with multiple meanings. So they insisted that any interpretations derived subjectively by the use of allegorizing must stay within the commonly accepted teachings of the church (i.e., within the "tradition" of the church). Jerome made a special point of emphasizing that allegorizing should

145

never be used to introduce any new doctrine or ever be *purely* subjective.

AUGUSTINE

SAYS = [MEANS¹]

MEANS²

MEANS³

MEANS⁴

Augustine went one step beyond those who preceded him and spoke of the four senses that a Scripture passage could have: the historical, the moral, the allegorical, and the analogical meanings. This eventually became the standard for interpretation throughout the Middle Ages up to the time of the Reformation.

To his credit, Augustine did not dismiss the literal meaning (Means¹) as Philo and Origen had done. He insisted that the historical sense of a passage was its basic meaning and all the other meanings had to be based on it.

Augustine also agreed with Jerome that the Bible must always be interpreted within the doctrinal bounds set by the church. Any interpretation that did not meet this doctrinal standard had to be suppressed. It is interesting to note that even though these two church leaders felt very keenly the danger of allegorizing and warned against its abuses, they still used it freely.

The warnings these men gave were well founded. Allegorizing does allow an interpreter to say all kinds of things that have little or nothing to do with the simple, plain meaning of the Bible passage that is supposedly being explained. The following example shows clearly how Augustine himself fell into this trap. Note how subjective his explanation of the parable of the good Samaritan is. The literal meaning of the words and the real lesson of the parable get lost in the fanciful meaning he assigns to almost every detail of this Scripture passage.

Augustine explains the parable of the good Samaritan like this⁴: The man going down from Jerusalem to Jericho is Adam. The thieves are the devil and his angels who stripped Adam of immortality. The beating the man suffered is the devil persuading Adam to sin, and when the man is left half dead, this is supposed to picture Adam's fallen state in which he still has some hope of life in the promise of the Savior.

The priest and the Levite, Augustine says, are the priesthood and the ministry of the Old Testament, which do not help anyone find salvation. The Samaritan is a picture of Jesus. The binding of the man's wounds is any action that prevents sin from being done. The oil is the comfort of hope, and the wine is the Lord's urging us to work with zeal. The beast on which the man was carried to the inn is the human body in which our Lord chose to come to us. Putting the man on the beast is faith in the incarnation of Christ.

The inn is the church where travelers are refreshed on their way to the heavenly country. The next day when the Samaritan left is the time after Christ's ascension. The two silver coins are either the two laws of love (love of God and love of neighbor) or the promise of this life and the life to come in heaven. The innkeeper is the apostle Paul. The offer of the Samaritan to pay any extra costs is Paul's encouragement (to those who can do so) to remain celibate.

This passage really is Jesus' answer to the question "Who is my neighbor?" By this parable Jesus shows that our neighbor is anyone in need. What the parable really teaches gets completely lost in Augustine's subjective allegorizing of the details of the parable. This example clearly demonstrates the problem with allegorizing. It is not interpretation. It is merely the interpreter's imagination at work.

The Middle Ages and the Renaissance

Eight hundred years after Augustine, allegorizing was still going strong, and four meanings were still being assigned to a passage of Scripture. Thomas Aquinas (d. 1274) agreed with Augustine that the literal meaning of a passage was the most important meaning, but he also indulged in multiple interpretations. For example, Aquinas said that God's command in creation, "Let there be light!", was first of all an act of creation. But he also gave these words three additional meanings: (1) Morally, it told the Christian what to do, namely, let the love of Christ shine in his life; (2) Allegorically, it told the Christian what to believe, namely, that he is spiritually illumined by Christ; and (3) Analogically, it told the Christian what to hope, namely, that he would be led by Christ to the light of eternal glory.

But in the Middle Ages the subjectivity of allegorizing was reaching new heights. Four meanings were assigned not only to passages but also to individual words. *Jerusalem* could be understood to be referring to the city, or it could be taken to mean "a faithful Christian" or "the church militant" or "the church triumphant." Eventually words took on not only four but limitless meanings according to the whim of the interpreter. Thus the word *sea* could mean almost anything a person decided: water, Scripture, the present age, the human heart, an active life, the heathen, or baptism.[5]

MIDDLE AGES

Individual words are also given four meanings.

The ground rules were still the same as those laid down by Jerome and Augustine. An allegorical interpretation was supposed to remain within the boundaries of the official doctrine of the church. This meant that the most honored interpreter was the one who could find new ways of supporting the teachings of the church by allegorizing.

Allegorizing opened the door for new doctrines to be introduced.

As the interpretation done in the Middle Ages moved slowly but surely away from the literal meaning of the inspired words to the subjective results of allegorizing, the door was also opened for new teachings to creep in. This was not supposed to happen according to the ground rules, but Satan was not about to miss the opportunity provided by the subjective interpretation that allegorizing not only allowed but even encouraged.

One example from the pen of Thomas Aquinas illustrates this point. Isaiah 11:1 says, "There shall come forth a rod out of the stem of Jesse" (KJV). Aquinas said "a rod" means the virgin Mary. Then he took a number of other passages in which the word rod was used and said they described what Mary does for Christians. Moses' rod was used to divide the

Red Sea, so Mary is one who consoles Christians in tribulation. Aaron's rod budded, so Mary makes Christians fruitful with good deeds. Moses' rod was used to draw water from a rock for Israel, so Mary gives Christians comfort in their trials. Since a rod was used to smite the corners of Moab, Mary also scourges Christians when they sin.[6]

When Aquinas and other medieval scholastic theologians added the dialectic method of Aristotle to this kind of fanciful allegorizing, the results were insufferable. Using Aristotle's categories, the content of a Bible passage would be arranged in a systematic form that had endless subdivisions: objections, solutions, definitions, corollaries, propositions, proofs, replies, reasons, refutations, exceptions, and distinctions. From these categories theses and antitheses would be developed, and the interpreter would carry out his argumentation mainly in syllogisms. Not surprisingly, interpretation of this kind combined with allegorizing led to results such as these: (1) Langenstein wrote four large volumes on the first four chapters of Genesis; (2) Hasselbach wrote 24 books that covered the interpretation of only the first chapter of Isaiah.[7]

The dialectic method of the Scholastics added to allegorizing led to pure madness.

These are extremes, to be sure, but they do illustrate the natural result when subjectivity is introduced into biblical interpretation. Satan will see to it that such subjective interpretation leads as far away as possible from the real meaning of the words of Scripture.

The Reformation

In the Reformation, the centuries of movement of interpretation away from the plain, simple meaning of the words of Scripture was reversed. Instead of looking for four meanings in every passage, inter-

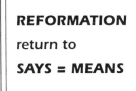

REFORMATION return to SAYS = MEANS

preters returned to the single, fundamental meaning *(usus simplex sensus)* of individual words and passages.

Luther disavowed the use of allegory as a legitimate tool of interpretation. A few of his remarks make this quite clear. An interpreter, he said, must avoid allegory "so that he does not wander into idle dreams." He called allegories empty speculations and the scum of Scripture. On one occasion he likened Pope Gregory I (one of the fathers of the medieval church and a strong proponent of allegorizing) to a beautiful prostitute who proves especially attractive to idle men. To him allegories were awkward, absurd, invented, obsolete, loose rags.[8]

This does not mean that Luther, especially in his early years, never allegorized. It was not easy for him to rid himself of a method that had predominated for such a long time in the church. But what he said about allegorizing makes it clear that he viewed allegorical interpretation of any kind as invalid.

This fact is also underscored by the principles of interpretation he championed in the Reformation, most of which are incompatible with allegorical interpretation:

1. Bible interpretation is to be done on the basis of the original languages rather than on the basis of the Latin Vulgate.

2. The interpreter should know the historical background of the books of the Bible rather than creating his own allegorical settings.

3. The interpreter must accept the unity of the entire Bible rather than allegorizing individual passages according to his own fanciful imagination.

4. The interpreter must begin with Christ as the center of Scripture in his interpretation of any part of the Bible.

5. Scripture must be interpreted by Scripture rather than be subject to any standard of doctrine (tradition) established by the leaders of the church.

Luther also applied the scriptural doctrine of the universal priesthood of all believers to the matter of interpretation. He encouraged lay people to read and interpret Scripture for themselves rather than being bound to any interpretation imposed on them by popes and bishops. By this Luther did not mean that each person had the freedom to interpret Scripture any way he wanted to. Like his pastor, every lay person was also bound to let Scripture interpret Scripture.

This restoration of the freedom for each Christian to read Scripture daily was a hallmark of the Reformation. As people read the simple, clear words of the Bible for themselves, they soon realized what Scripture actually taught about God's free gift of forgiveness. This, perhaps more than anything else, helped free consciences from the cruel bonds of the error of self-righteousness which had bean imposed on the church especially during the Middle Ages by the papacy.

A historical-critical view
of Luther and Bible interpretation

Some contemporary Lutherans who espouse the historical-critical method of interpretation mistakenly claim Luther as their model. They twist Luther's words to give the impression that Luther did not consider the Scripture to be the Word of God, or that he did not believe the Bible was verbally inspired and inerrant, or that he felt the Word of God was not contained in Scripture alone. Anyone who hears such claims about Luther would be well advised to read the context of the quotes on which these claims are based. Reading the wider context of these quotes always shows that Luther is being misrepresented by the people who ascribe these beliefs to him.[9]

Contemporary historical-critical Lutherans also praise Luther for formulating some "new" principles of interpretation for his day. This is a half-truth that again misrepresents Luther. Yes, Luther did reject the multiple meanings for Bible passages that were the result of allegorizing, and so he did introduce a way of interpretation that was different from what had been used for centuries prior to the Reformation. The historical-critical Lutherans of our day say that they are doing for the church today what Luther did for the church in his day.

What they refuse to recognize is the fact that Luther's interpretation was not new. Rather, it was a rejection of allegorizing and a return to the only way that Scripture can properly be interpreted, letting SAYS = MEANS. Actually, the historical-critical Lutherans of our day are doing just the opposite of what Luther did. As will be illustrated later in chapter 10, they are rejecting the way of interpretation that lets SAYS = MEANS and turning to a new and more subtle kind of allegorizing that the devil has devised to mislead the church today. In short, Luther's "new" way of interpretation restored proper interpretation; the contemporary historical-critical Lutherans' "new" way of interpretation takes people away from the proper form of interpretation. They can hardly claim Luther as their hero just because they are going a new way in interpretation.

Luther's "new" way of interpretation was really a return to the only proper way of interpretation.

What makes this even more evident is the attitude of these modern Lutherans toward the principles of interpretation that Luther restored. Luther, they say, was a medieval man with a medieval mentality. He accepted all the miracles taught in the Bible. He accepted the Bible's presentation that many of the events of the Old Testament, in Christ's life, and in the spread of the early church were the result of God's hand guiding history. Such a person, they argue, could not be expected to contribute much to solving the problems that interpretation poses in our modern, scientific age. Note that they do not acknowledge Luther as one who interpreted Scripture correctly. They only want to use his name as a front to promote the new method of interpretation that they prefer.

Calvin, Roman Catholicism

John Calvin (d. 1564) followed many of the same principles of interpretation that Luther did. There was one major difference, however. When Scripture says something that is difficult or even impossible for human reason to grasp (e.g., predestination, the real presence in the Lord's Supper, the two natures of Christ), Luther insisted that what Scripture says must be what it means, even though it may not be able to be fully understood. Calvin, on the other hand, felt that any such matter should be interpreted in a way that the meaning of the words was comprehensible to human reason.

Calvin felt this way because he insisted on the absolute clarity of all of Scripture. But this is not a proper application of the truth that Scripture is clear. The problem is not with Scripture. Scripture is not unclear in what it says and means when, for example, it speaks about the fact that Christ is true God and true man in one person. The problem is with us human beings. We are not always able to grasp fully some of the wonderful things God does with his almighty power. The solution to the problem in cases like this is not to change the meaning of the Bible to fit our reason. Instead, the only proper solution is to let the meaning of Scripture stand and in faith to rejoice in what God in his power does to bring the blessings of his grace to us.

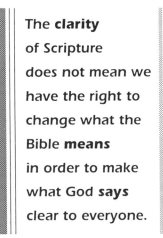

The clarity of Scripture does not mean we have the right to change what the Bible means in order to make what God says clear to everyone.

The Roman Catholic approach to biblical interpretation was firmly established at the Council of Trent (1545-1563). The Lutheran watchword for doing interpretation, *sola Scriptura* (by Scripture alone), was condemned. For Roman Catholic interpreters, the tradition of the church (i.e., interpretations of Scripture endorsed officially by the pope and the bishops in a church council) was made an equal partner with the Bible. The tradition of the Roman Catholic Church often conflicts with the clear statements of Scripture. So this decision of the Council of Trent (which still stands as the official position of Roman Catholicism) placed error on the same footing as truth in doing biblical interpretation.

Post-Reformation interpretation

The doctrinal controversies that arose between Lutheranism and Roman Catholicism on the one hand, and between Lutheranism and the Reformed churches on the other hand, led to an intensive study of Scripture in

Lutheranism. The fruits of these studies are the Lutheran Confessions and other doctrinal writings that are invaluable for true Lutherans to this day.

Even a brief glance at the intensive study of the Bible done by Lutherans in the post-Reformation period reveals that Luther's basic principle of interpretation was still being followed. The fundamental rule of Lutheran interpretation continued to be that Scripture is the only true interpreter of Scripture. The Lutheran theologians of this period insisted that nothing be taught contrary to the sum total of what is set forth in all the statements of Scripture that clearly deal with the specific matter under discussion. This is sometimes referred to as "the analogy of faith."

Many of the Lutheran doctrinal writings of this time (which grew out of a careful and proper interpretation of what Scripture says and means) contained both theses and antitheses. This was done to express doctrine as clearly as possible, both by setting forth what Scripture taught, as well as by denying what Scripture does not teach on a given subject.

> **Doctrinal confessions are necessary, but they should never be used as a substitute for the Bible itself.**

However, as time went by an unhealthy tendency developed. Some Lutherans began to resort to those doctrinal formulations as the first line of defense against false teachings. They would look to the Lutheran Confessions as the authority to settle any and all doctrinal controversies, instead of addressing a doctrinal issue on the basis of Scripture first of all. This in turn contributed to a gradual neglect of a continual, intensive study of the Scriptures themselves.

Doctrinal formulations, no matter how well they state a doctrine and no matter how firmly they are based on the proper interpretation of Scripture, should not be consistently quoted in preference to, or more often than, Scripture itself in doctrinal discussions. Nor should quotations from the Lutheran Confessions ever be considered all that Scripture has to say on a doctrinal matter. Simply put, doctrinal formulations are misused when they become a ready-made theology that is used as a substitute for a careful study of Scripture.

Summary

In the early Christian church, the devil was able, slowly but surely, to undermine the truth of God's Word. One of the means by which he accomplished this was the gradual introduction of allegorizing into the interpretation of Scripture. Those who used allegorizing did not necessarily intend to introduce false doctrine into the teachings of the church. Nevertheless, the subjectivity, which is an essential part of allegorizing, proved to be a tool in Satan's service to do just that.

In the Reformation, Luther did not introduce a new method of interpretation. Rather, God guided the restoration of the one and only way in which the saving truths of his Word can be rightly understood and continually preserved against the onslaughts of error. This method was to let the meaning derived from a passage by interpretation be the same as what the words simply and plainly said.

Doctrinal statements derived from the proper interpretation of Scripture are not only helpful but also often absolutely necessary to help distinguish the truth of God's Word from Satan's errors. However, doctrinal formulations should never be used as a substitute for the continual study of Scripture itself.

NOTES

1. *Interpreter's Bible* (Nashville: Abingdon Press, 1952), Vol. 1, p. 108.

2. F. W. Farrar, *History of Interpretation* (Grand Rapids: Baker Book House, 1961), p. 150.

3. F. W. Farrar, *op. cit.,* p. 199.

4. Augustine, Questionum Evangeliorum, II, 19 (*Petrologgiae Cursus Completus*, XXXV).

5. Interpreter's Bible, Vol. 1, p. 122.

6. F. W. Farrar, *op. cit.*, p. 288.

7. F. W. Farrar, *op. cit.*, p. 289.

8. F. W. Farrar, *op. cit.*, p. 328.

9. S. W. Becker, "Luther's Concept of the Word of God," *Wisconsin Lutheran Quarterly,* Vol. 64, pp. 82-100,193-212, and

D. Kuske, "Luther and the Historical-Critical Method of Interpretation in the Lutheran Church," *Luther Lives* (Milwaukee: Northwestern Publishing House, 1983), pp. 131-143.

BIBLIOGRAPHY—CHAPTER EIGHT

Dockery, D. S. *Biblical interpretation—Then and Now.* Grand Rapids: Baker Book House, 1992.

Farrar, F. W. *History of Interpretation.* Grand Rapids: Baker Book House, 1961. pp. 98-293.

Mickelsen, A. B. *Interpreting the Bible.* Grand Rapids: William B. Eerdmans Publishing Co., 1963. pp. 20-47.

Oswald, H. C., and G. S. Robbert (compilers). *Luther as Interpreter of Scripture.* St. Louis: Concordia Publishing House, 1982.

Zuck, R. B. *Basic Bible Interpretation.* Wheaton, IL: Scripture Press-Victor Books, 1991. pp. 27-58.

9

PIETISM, RATIONALISM, AND EXISTENTIALISM

Lutheran Pietism

In the post-Reformation period, Lutherans were genuinely concerned about holding on to the true doctrine, which God had restored in the Reformation. In the 17th century, however, two historical developments led to circumstances that helped bring about a breakdown in the spiritual life of the church.

First, constant warfare raged across Germany during the Thirty Years War (1618-1648). This made congregational life almost non-existent for many Lutheran churches. The spiritual life of the church went downhill quickly without the strengthening and encouragement provided by fellow Christians gathering regularly around God's Word. Second, the organization of territorial churches after the Thirty Years War automatically made any person living in a certain area a member of the church of that area. In the Lutheran territories, this meant that people were Lutheran by birth rather than by conviction and a profession of faith. This automatic church membership led people to take spiritual matters less seriously and so also contributed to the weakening of the spiritual life of the church.

Pietism was a religious movement that developed with the aim of improving the spiritual life of the church. Pietists felt that a third factor had contributed to the sad condition of the church. They were sure that the importance of sanctification had been overlooked in the desire to ensure doctrinal purity in the post-Reformation period. The cure, they insisted, was to develop a more emotional Christianity.[1]

This attempt to bring about a more emotional Christianity also led to a new approach to Bible interpretation. Lutheran pietists began to disregard the basic Lutheran principle of letting Scripture interpret Scripture. Instead, the personal emotions of the interpreter became the most important factor in determining the meaning of a Bible passage. Pietists felt that a Christian should always be looking for a meaning in a passage that would move him to show love for God in his life. This meant that the *objective* meaning of a passage was less important than what an individual might discover *subjectively* to stir him to live a life more devoted to God.

PIETISM SAYS = MEANS (what moves a person to live a more pious life)

In this process, some pietists considered it important to try to feel what the emotions of the biblical writer were when he wrote a specific passage. If a person was sure his feelings were in harmony with those of the inspired writer, and if this mystical relationship with the biblical writer resulted in an interpretation that led the pietist to glorify God in his life, then it was felt that no one could deny this was the best meaning of that passage for that person.

Some pietists were very careful not to permit this emotional, subjective element in Bible interpretation to take them too far away from the simple, plain meaning of the words. Other more radical pietists became very subjective and believed they were directly illuminated by the Holy Spirit. They felt that their personal interpretations were the result of an "inner light" that made their interpretation the right one not only for themselves but also for others.

Whether it was the work of such radical pietists or those less radical, all the interpretation done by pietists included an element of subjectivity. This cancer inevitably ate away at the objective truth of Scripture because once Satan has his foot in the door he will not stop there. The growing subjectivity in interpretation introduced by pietism left the church weak and unable to counter successfully the onslaught of rationalistic interpretation, which was totally subjective.

Rationalism's denial of the supernatural

A basic tenet of rationalism is that something is real only if it can be verified by modern methods of research. Whatever does not lie within the realm of human experience can't be real, the rationalist insists. Or to put it another way, the supernatural is impossible. This denial of the supernatural affects the rationalist's view of the Bible in two ways. His view of

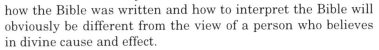

RATIONALISM

The supernatural is impossible.

how the Bible was written and how to interpret the Bible will obviously be different from the view of a person who believes in divine cause and effect.

Since divine revelation involves the supernatural, the rationalist denies that the Bible could have come into existence by divine revelation. Verbal inspiration and inerrancy simply do not exist. In place of these two truths taught by Scripture, rationalism proposes some different theories about how the Bible came into being and what kind of book it is. These theories in one way or another all make the Bible a purely human book.

In the 1800s, one of the more popular theories about the Bible among rationalists was that it was written by men who had deeper religious insight than most people have. Therefore, they considered what the biblical writers said to be worth far more than the thoughts of any ordinary religious person.

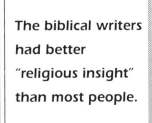

The biblical writers had better "religious insight" than most people.

This point can be illustrated by a comparison with other fields of study. The men who study science or history as their life's work obviously know more about these subjects than most other people. In the same way, it is argued, the biblical writers had keener religious insights than most people. However, just like the best scientist or historian, the biblical writers were human and so they were subject to error.

Another popular theory among 19th-century rationalists was the idea of the progressive or evolutionary advance of truth in religion. This theory said that like any other field of human study, there were at first some basic religious truths that were mixed with many errors or misunderstandings. But man in his constant search for "truth" is constantly sorting things out for himself. By this sorting, man gradually moves from a state of much error and little truth to a state of less error and more truth. Through the Old Testament into the New, this theory says, one can see this development taking place. The final stage of truth was not reached in the New Testament, but it goes on as part of man's search for truth in each new generation.

The human experience contributes to the constant advance of "religious truth."

In either of these theories, the rationalist maintains that a person can use Scripture at best only as a starting point in his own personal search for religious truth. In the process of this search, each succeeding generation contributes to the development of religious truth and so makes the search easier for subsequent generations.

Rationalistic Bible interpretation

The denial of the supernatural—and, therefore, of verbal inspiration and the inerrancy of Scripture—naturally affected how the rationalist interpreted the Bible. In the 1800s it was commonly held that the only acceptable religious truths in the Bible were those that could be explained by natural cause and effect. Those events in the Bible that the writers ascribed to divine cause and effect were explained away by the use of a distinction borrowed from the study of secular history.

160

The distinction made in the study of history at 19th-century German universities was a distinction between historical facts *(Historie)* and the interpretation of historical facts *(Geschichte).* This is a proper distinction that needs to be made in any study of the events of history. For example, these are some facts *(Historie)* about the First World War: (1) It was fought from 1914 to 1918; (2) Germany and France were on opposing sides in this war; (3) Toward the end of the war, United States soldiers went to Europe to fight in this war. When a person reads about the First World War in history books, one needs to distinguish between facts such as these *(Historie)* and the interpretation of the facts by historians *(Geschichte).* An example of the latter would be the various reasons that historians give why the war started, why Germany lost, etc. Historians often disagree in matters such as these since they are judgments made by scholars on the basis of the facts.

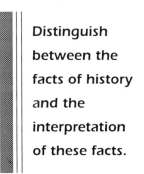

Distinguish between the facts of history and the interpretation of these facts.

As was said earlier, this distinction, which is in and of itself a proper one, was carried over by rationalists into the interpretation of Scripture. Rationalists said that passages containing anything supernatural were fictitious additions made by early Christians to portray Christ as a superhero.[2]

Sometimes these interpretations *(Geschichte)* were dismissed as being of little or no importance for the modern reader. At other times, the accounts about Jesus' miracles were given naturalistic or mythical interpretations. For example, the resurrection of Jesus was explained as reviving from a faint (or maybe a coma) after a time of quiet rest in the cooler temperature of the tomb. The miracle of the wedding of Cana, rationalists said, taught the inspiring religious truth that an ordinary life (represented by the water) can be changed into a special life (represented by the wine).

Rationalists ascribed the accounts about supernatural events in the life of Jesus to the primitive, non-scientific worldview of the early church. Ancient people believed there were gods and demons who could influence human events. This, the rationalist argued, is what led biblical writers to speak about Jesus doing miracles.

"Proof" that the Bible is the product of a primitive worldview

As "proof" that the Bible came into being as the product of a primitive worldview, the rationalist points to "facts" that can be established by the study of religion in primitive groups of people in the world today. Look, the rationalist says, at some of the Eskimos or some of the tribes in Africa or South America. By studying such people, the rationalist insists, a person will be able to document how all religions and sacred books, including the Bible, come into existence.

The supernatural is part of an ancient, non-scientific worldview.

The first stage of religion in primitive groups is the development of religious myths. In these myths, many things are ascribed to the actions of gods and demons. These myths may have a grain of truth in them, but as primitive people develop the ability to learn more about the world around them by methods of scientific investigation, these myths are abandoned. What replaces them are religious "truths" that are based more and more on natural cause and effect.

The conclusion that the rationalist draws from this "proof" of how all religions develop is that the Bible is helpful only in the sense that it makes a contribution to the study of how religious thought develops. To every rationalist the Bible is a thoroughly human book, subject to all the strengths and weaknesses of human insights gained from the study of human experience.

Rationalistic literary criticism

Rationalists used the study of the development of primitive religions as a scientific base to assist them in interpreting the synoptic gospels (Matthew, Mark, Luke). They felt they could identify the sources from which the gospels evolved by comparing these gospels with what was learned from contemporary primitive religions.

The goal of identifying these sources was to put the Bible interpreter in a better position to determine the origin of the gospels. Knowing the sources of these writings would help the interpreter separate the facts of history *(Historie)* from the strands of subjective interpretation *(Geschichte),* which, the rationalist said, the people of the early church had interwoven with the historical facts.

In following this approach, rationalistic literary criticism identified three successive stages through which each of the synoptic gospels was supposed to have passed before it evolved into a final product. These three stages will be briefly described in the next three portions of this chapter. No attempt will be made to explain each stage in depth. Rather, the main goal will be to show what this evolution of the synoptic gospels allows the interpreter to do. It allows him to question and eliminate almost anything and everything he chooses. The dates given do not represent any one view, but they represent a composite view developed on the basis of what a number of writers have said on this subject.[3]

Form criticism

The first stage in the development of the synoptic gospels according to rationalistic literary criticism was the oral stage. The study of this stage is called *form criticism.* It is called this because its proponents assume that as stories about Jesus were repeated, they took on certain forms according to the original setting of a particular story. One story that was repeated might have been part of a sermon, another might have been used in the liturgy, and still another might have been used in a teaching situation.

If identifying these forms were a scientific process, as rationalists insist, then one would expect that they would all agree on how many forms there are and exactly what the essential characteristic of each form is. This isn't the case. The following is just one theory among many about how the oral forms could be categorized. In this theory two main categories of forms are suggested: the sayings and the narratives.

The sayings form was subdivided in two ways. The first type is simply a saying of Jesus with nothing accompanying it. The second type is a saying of Jesus that has a story made up to accompany that saying. For example, it is said that the story of the Pharisee and the publican was never spoken by Jesus. Rather, this story was added to accompany Jesus' saying about the proud being humbled and the humble being exalted.

The narratives form was also subdivided in two ways. A miracle story is a type of narrative that the rationalist says is not historical. Rather, it is a story made up by people in the early church. A legend is a narrative such as Jesus' passion (which might be somewhat historical) or the story about his resurrection, which, like the miracle stories, is not considered historical at all.

Form criticism rests on the assumption that for about 30 to 50 years after Jesus' death (A.D. 30 to 80) isolated incidents from Jesus' life and snatches of his teachings were repeated orally by Christians. It was only later that anything of substance was written down. Some say this process went on for more than a century before the written stage began.

It is also assumed that these oral traditions were independent, self-contained stories, or *pericopes,* about Jesus. Those who repeated these stories were not primarily interested in giving facts about Jesus' life. Their main goal was to give an interpretation of Jesus' life from the viewpoint of their faith in him. Jesus was something that went way beyond the ordinary, and this was the way they wanted others to learn to know Jesus.

As Jesus' followers told others what Jesus meant for them, some facts about Jesus' life were *preserved* in the stories that were told. The Sermon on the Mount is a possible example of a preservation. Jesus actually may have said part or much of what is included in Matthew 5-7. However, many of the facts were either *interpreted* or *transformed.* An example of an interpretation are those passages in which Jesus is said to be the Savior from sin. That (they say) clearly is not what Jesus said, but it is an interpretation of what he said by the early

Christians. An example of a transformation might be the feeding of the 5,000. What actually happened that day was that the boy who had the bread and the fish offered to share it with the others in the crowd. People who were hiding some food that they had brought along followed this young lad's example and also shared their food. So everyone was fed. This "fact" was transformed into a miracle story. Some "facts" were even *created*. The illustration given earlier of the story of the Pharisee and the publican being created to accompany Jesus' saying about the humble and the proud is an example.

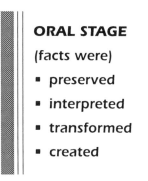

ORAL STAGE

(facts were)

- **preserved**

- **interpreted**

- **transformed**

- **created**

By identifying the forms in which these stories appear in the gospels, one is supposed to be able to determine whether a given passage is the result of preservation, interpretation, transformation, or creation in the oral stage. This in turn determines whether it is actually a historical fact *(Historie)* or only an idea that came from the minds and imagination of the early Christians *(Geschichte)*.

Again, if this were a scientific process, one would expect that rationalistic literary critics would agree in their analysis of most passages. But often there are as many different opinions as there are critics. Thus this first stage casts a cloud of doubt over most of the words and events recorded in the synoptics. Are they historical or not? The answer is not clear at all. The matter is left for each "scholar" to decide based on his theory of what form a particular passage took in the oral stage of development. But this is really only the beginning. There are still two more stages of development that the gospels were supposed to have gone through that make the answer to this question even more muddled.

Source criticism

The second stage of development, rationalists say, was the written stage. This stage is supposed to have taken place in a period from roughly A.D. 60 to 120.

The study of this stage is called *source criticism* because it is assumed that gradually the independent stories of the oral stage were gathered into a number of written documents. These written documents are said to be the main sources from which the synoptic gospels, as we know them, developed. Rationalistic criticism claims that the problem of how these gospels ended up being both so similar and so different at the same time is solved by identifying the sources from which each gospel evolved.

Some say that there were only two sources: Ur-Markus and Q (*Quelle,* which is a German word meaning source). Others say there were four sources: Ur-Markus, Q, M, and L.

The four-source theory goes like this:

1. Ur-Markus is identified as a written document that gradually evolved into the gospel of Mark.

2. Either Ur-Markus or Mark in turn is one of the sources from which Matthew and Luke developed. This is supposed to explain why Mark, Matthew, and Luke all have some material that is similar.

3. Another document, Q (which it is assumed was mainly a collection of sayings of Jesus), is suggested as a second source for Matthew and Luke. Since Q was not used by Mark, this is supposed to explain why Matthew and Luke have some sayings of Jesus that are not in Mark.

4. The material in Matthew that neither Luke nor Mark has is supposed to have come from a document called M. The material in Luke that neither Matthew nor Mark has came from a document L. This "explains" why Matthew and Luke each have material that neither of the other synoptic gospels has.

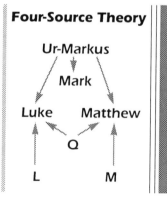

Four-Source Theory

Ur-Markus

Mark

Luke   Matthew

Q

L   M

If this theory were truly scientific, one would expect that the scholars would basically agree what the content of the original sources was. This is not the case.

Each scholar has his own idea about what part of the synoptic gospels came from Ur-Markus, or Q, or L and M.

Nor do these scholars have any explanation, if there were such written documents such as these, why there is no mention of them in any of the historical writings of the early Christian church. Surely one could expect that the early church fathers would have said something about these sources if they had really existed. Wouldn't these men—who lived at the time when this written stage of the New Testament was supposedly talking place and who said so many other things about the New Testament—have said at least a little something about the sources from which their sacred book was evolving during their lifetime?

The fact that there is no mention of these sources in the writings of the early church fathers, together with the fact that the scholars can't agree on what these sources supposedly contained, indicates that these sources are figments of their imagination.

In spite of these problems, rationalistic literary critics insist that their theory is scientific and that the synoptics evolved in this way in this second stage. Furthermore, they say that the processes that took place in the oral stage repeated themselves in the written stage. Some of the oral forms were *preserved.* Others were *interpreted* or *transformed.* And some of the material that appeared in this second stage did not come from the oral stage at all. Christians also added to the life of Jesus by *creating* new "facts" as they wrote the oral stories down.

This means that anyone reading the gospels today has quite a thicket to find his way through if he wants to find anything historical. He will have to decide if he is reading a preservation (written stage) of an interpretation or transformation or creation from the oral stage. Or he might be reading a transformation (written stage) of an interpretation or transformation or creation from the oral stage. Or he might be reading an interpretation (written stage) of a preservation or interpretation or transformation or creation from the oral stage. Only if he decides he is reading a preservation (written stage) of a preservation from the oral stage can he assume that maybe he is reading something historical about Jesus.

Obviously, a heavier cloud of doubt has been cast over historicity of the synoptic gospels and their account of Jesus' life. But the end is not yet. There is still more that makes any certainty even more remote.

Redaction criticism

The third stage of development, according to rationalistic literary criticism, is the editorial stage. This stage is dated anywhere from A.D. 80 to 160. How did the fragments of stories about Jesus from the oral stage, and the haphazard sources that gathered the stories from the oral stage into a written form, end up in an orderly book such as Matthew, Mark, and Luke? Somebody, the rationalistic literary critics say, had to have a general plan that he used to put the oral fragments and written sources into the order that we have them today. It is assumed, therefore, that there must have been editors who put the whole book together. These editors were called redactors. The study of what they did is called *redaction criticism.*

But the redactor did not just arrange the material. He is also supposed to have *added* things, or *interpreted* things as he saw fit, or *emphasized or de-emphasized* things from his own perspective. He also *created* temporal, geographical, ideal, or typical contexts into which he placed the material he took from the oral forms and written sources. For example, geographical settings were added that are symbolical rather than historical: (1) Galilee in Mark's gospel is always associated with Gentile Christianity; (2) In Luke the desert is associated with temptation, the mountain with Jesus speaking with the Father, the open plain with crowds of people, and the sea with supernatural power.[4] In other words, the events recorded in these gospels did not necessarily happen at these geographical locations. The redactor

EDITORIAL STAGE

(oral & written material was)

- added
- interpreted
- emphasized or de-emphasized
- created

added them to try to give a special theological slant to each passage.

This means that the interpreter has another layer of human additions to find his way through in order to get back to the historical Jesus. He may be reading an addition (editorial stage) to an interpretation (written stage) of a transformation in the oral stage. Or a passage might be a de-emphasizing (editorial stage) of a transformation (written stage) of a creation in the oral stage. Or any other number of combinations of the various processes that were supposed to have taken place in each of the stages of the development of the gospels.

But even this is not the end. There is still more that adds to the doubt that rationalistic literary criticism casts over the historical nature of the gospels. The fourth element that was supposed to have influenced the development of the gospels is religion criticism.

Religion criticism

This fourth item in the development of the gospels is not a fourth stage in the sequence. Rather, it is assumed that in all three stages described in the preceding paragraphs there was a fourth influence continually at work.

Various religious philosophies of the time are said to have been incorporated into what people said in the oral forms, into what was written in the four sources, and into what the redactor put together as the final product. The study of the religious ideas that were included by people at all three stages is called religion criticism.

If any of the statements in the gospels ascribed to Jesus are similar to what is found in the rabbinical writings, it is assumed that these are not things that Jesus said. Instead, they are considered additions made in one of the three stages as the result of the influence of Jewish religious thought. If there is any "story" in the gospels (such as the

ALL THREE STAGES
Jewish and Hellenistic ideas creep in.

virgin birth) that is similar to what is found in Greek literature, it is assumed that this story was added as the result of Greek religious thought. The idea of the virgin birth is supposed to have come from the Greek myths in which the Greek gods had intercourse with human women and produced some superhuman heroes.

MODERN VIEW OF THE GOSPELS

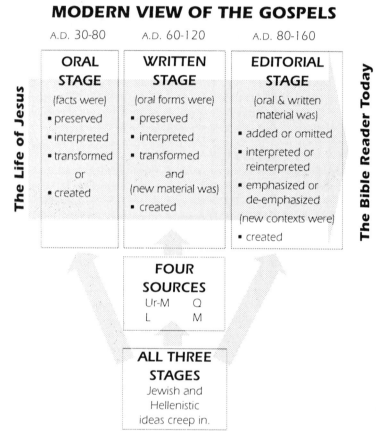

A.D. 30-80   A.D. 60-120   A.D. 80-160

The Life of Jesus

ORAL STAGE	WRITTEN STAGE	EDITORIAL STAGE
(facts were)	(oral forms were)	(oral & written material was)
• preserved	• preserved	• added or omitted
• interpreted	• interpreted	• interpreted or reinterpreted
• transformed or	• transformed and	• emphasized or de-emphasized
• created	(new material was)	(new contexts were)
	• created	• created

The Bible Reader Today

FOUR SOURCES

Ur-M   Q

L   M

ALL THREE STAGES

Jewish and
Hellenistic
ideas creep in.

This chart shows how rationalistic literary criticism views the synoptic gospels. The life of Jesus supposedly went through three revisions during the centuries after Christ lived. At each stage of this evolution (oral, written, editorial) the early church modified the record of Jesus' life in various ways as indicated. The Bible reader today, then, cannot be sure of what is historical fact or what is the result of the kerygma ("preaching") of the early church.

A brief analysis of rationalistic literary criticism

This form of literary criticism is called "scientific" and "scholarly" by its radical supporters. It is also called "neutral" or "not incompatible with" a believing study of the Bible by some who still want to be known as conservative Christians in our day.

But two things must be noted that put the lie to both of these claims:

1. This form of literary criticism begins with a totally rationalistic view of how the Bible came into being. Oral, source, redaction, and religious criticism are rooted in the denial that God had anything to do with the origin of Scripture. Instead, the Bible is considered a thoroughly human book.

2. Whoever uses oral, source, redaction, and religious criticism is going to place man above the Bible as the arbiter of what belongs in the Bible and what doesn't. Some will do it to a greater degree, others to a lesser degree—but all will do it to some degree. Those who do it to a greater degree say that much, if not all of the Bible is not historical. Those who do it to a lesser degree may say that only some of the Bible is not historical. But one doesn't have to be a prophet to know that this yeast of doubt will gradually spread, and more and more of the Bible will be considered unhistorical. In 1 Corinthians 5:6 and Galatians 5:9 God himself says that this is what Satan's yeast will always do.

Baur and Strauss

Ferdinand Baur and David Strauss were two 19th-century interpreters whose unique approaches are worth looking at briefly. Their ideas continue to be somewhat influential in the 20th century and are cited from time to time by those involved in interpreting Scripture from a rationalistic viewpoint.

Baur (d. 1860) suggested that the development of Christianity in the first century was the result of conflict between a Jewish Christianity, which Peter promoted, and a Gentile Christianity promoted by Paul. The story of Acts is supposed to represent how these two antithetical forms of Christianity were gradually molded together by compromise on the part of both groups. Baur dated and interpreted all the New Testament books according to his theory. This was done by determining at what stage in this conflict each New Testament book was written.

Strauss (d. 1874) wrote a book *(The Life of Jesus)* in which he suggested that the message of the gospels is expressed in mythical language. He defined mythical language as statements that are religiously true even though they may not be historical. He concluded that the best way to interpret any of the gospels was to concentrate on their religious content rather than on their historical content. For example, the interpreter should not concern himself whether there ever was a wedding at Cana that Jesus attended and whether Jesus changed water into wine there. Instead, the interpreter should concentrate on the religious truth that Jesus can change a person's life from something common like water into something special like good wine.

With this approach Strauss introduced the distinction between absolute truth and relative truth into the interpretation of God's Word. This distinction is very much a part of most kinds of historical-critical interpretation in our day. More will be said about it in the following chapters, which deal with contemporary types of interpretation that use rationalistic literary criticism.

Liberal theology

The growing use of rationalistic literary criticism in Bible interpretation had devastating results by the early 1900s. Since much of Scripture was considered human and not historical, the purpose of studying the Bible was reduced to maintaining morality among mankind.

Bible interpretation became a search for principles that govern the proper moral life. This liberal theology turned the gospel of the forgiveness of sins through Christ's redeeming work into a "social gospel." Jesus was reduced to a marvelous example of how people should love one another unselfishly. The books of the Bible were a prime source for people to evaluate their religious experiences and moral ideals.

Our reaction to this reduction of the Bible to a purely human book came from an unlikely source, the field of philosophy. Existentialism opposed rationalism and condemned what existentialists argued were the negative results of rationalism in people's daily lives. Some people also felt that existentialism was the answer to the negative results of rationalism in Bible interpretation and theology.

Rationalism opposed by existentialism

The negative literary criticism that grew out of rationalism was widespread in biblical interpretation throughout Europe by the end of the 19th century. But not everyone accepted it. Some of its better known opponents were Hengstenberg, Keil, Delitzsch, and Zahn. As was just noted, opposition also came from another source: existential philosophy.

Sören Kierkegaard (d. 1855) is generally considered one of the founders of existentialism. Kierkegaard held that religious faith is irrational. For him this meant that religious beliefs cannot be supported by rational arguments. He also rejected the claim of rationalism that what is real can always be investigated by modern scientific methods of research. This was especially true, Kierkegaard insisted, of God. He felt that God could only be known by faith.

Existentialists also had other views that are distinctly different from those of rationalists. The proponents of existentialism accused rationalism of minimizing the individuality of a human being and treating people as part of a mass. Existentialists said that the industrial revolution was not a step forward in man's development because people were being made to work at long assembly lines doing mindless tasks over and over again. Existentialists protested anything like rationalism and the industrial revolution, which treated people as if they were mere things and thus stifled the spontaneity and uniqueness of each individual.

Existentialism considers each individual's existence of far greater importance than the needs or desires of any given group of people. Therefore, it also distinguished sharply between subjective and objective truth. This is especially true in matters such as religion where the individual's "being"

(German: *Sein*) and his ultimate goal as an individual (his "authentic being") are involved.

EXISTENTIALISM

- **GOAL =**
  authentic being
- **TRUTH =**
  subjective
- **REALITY =**
  the present

Objective truth was considered less important since it can mean knowing things in an impersonal and detached way. Subjective truth is more important because it is truth that lays hold on an individual personally and affects him in everything in his life that involves his "being." Objective truth is also generally considered timeless, but, to the true existentialist, the present time is the only reality. Whatever is past or whatever is still to come is not of any real importance compared to a person's existence at the present moment.

Existentialism's goal is to help a person find what his true existence as a human being really is, his authentic being. This goal is not easy to reach because each human being is at the same time part of a world that does not allow him to exist as an individual. The world surrounds the individual and affects him in many ways. It tries to get him to consider the past and to worry about the future instead of focusing on the present. It tries to get him to think more about the groups of people of which he is part rather than of his own personal existence. It forces people to think about what is true in general for all people rather than what is true for them individually.

As a result a person's existence in the world makes his "being" ambiguous and sets one part of his "being" at odds with the other part:

- He is *free* but at the same time he is part of the world which makes him *unfree*.
- He is *finite*, but he is capable of becoming something more than he is at any given time. So he is also *infinite*.
- He is bound by *time*, but he is also part of *eternity*.

The existentialist believes that he can reach his goal of finding his "authentic being"—what he needs to become to be a free and finite human being—by wresting with the ambiguities that the world makes him face in each new situation in life. There are two key things he must always remember in order to succeed: (1) His real "being" is his existence as an individual; and (2) His present situation is the only real one, not anything in the past or in the future.

Summary

Pietism sought to right what was wrong in the church by introducing a type of biblical interpretation that was supposed to lead to a more pious life. In the process it opened the door for the totally subjective approach of rationalism.

In spite of insisting that all truth must be objectively determined, rationalism's denial of anything supernatural led to a type of interpretation that allowed a person to eliminate anything he wished. The rationalistic biblical interpreters who used oral, source, redaction, and religious criticism ended up saying that there was very little in the Bible about Jesus that was historical. The result of *rationalism* was a "gospel" that was only concerned about promoting love among mankind.

Existentialism insisted that God could be real to an individual even if he could not prove it scientifically. Existentialism introduced two ideas that were to prove very influential in much of 20th-century biblical interpretation: the search for "authentic being" and the present as the only reality.

All three of these movements were enemies of true biblical interpretation since all were based on some type of subjective interpretation, which places the interpreter in a position of authority over the Word of God as its judge. Pietism made the emotions and feelings of the interpreter decisive. Rationalism made the "scientific" judgment of the scholar decisive. Existentialism made the interpreter's finding of his authentic being decisive.

All paid lip service to the Bible as an important book, but then each proceeded to undermine Scripture's divine authorship and authority. Each introduced its own subjective context instead of staying with the objective meaning of the words in the context of Scripture itself.

NOTES

1. T. Hoyer, *The Story of the Church* (St. Louis: Concordia Publishing House, 1942), p. 104.

2. However, God says (2 Peter 1:20) that the men who wrote the Bible were inspired by him not only when they wrote historical facts (Jesus lived, died, rose, and ascended) but also when they interpreted these facts (the meaning of Jesus' redeeming work for us).

3. Most of the men who write about form, source, and redaction criticism do not give any exact dates. Instead, they basically operate with the assumption that Mark's gospel (or Ur-Markus) was the first on the scene about A.D. 70 and that this marks the beginning of the transition from the oral stage to the written stage. Most also agree that the redactors did not do their work until several decades of the second century had passed. In 1976, John A. T. Robinson wrote a book (*Redating the New Testament,* Philadelphia: Westminster Press) in which he maintained that all the New Testament books were written before the destruction of Jerusalem in A.D. 70. He insisted that his approach does not invalidate the stages of the development of the New Testament according to critical scholarship. It only shrinks the time frame that is usually suggested.

4. S. Kistemaker, *The Gospels in Current Study* (Grand Rapids: Baker Book House, 1972), p. 188.

BIBLIOGRAPHY—CHAPTER NINE

Anderson, C. *Critical Quests of Jesus.* Grand Rapids: William B. Eerdmans Publishing Co., 1970.

_____ . *The Historical Jesus: A Continuing Quest.* Grand Rapids: William B. Eerdmans Publishing Co., 1972.

Black, A. B., and D. S. Dockery (eds.). *New Testament Criticism and Interpretation.* Grand Rapids: Zondervan Publishing Corporation, 1991. Chapters 5-7, pp. 137-226.

Briggs, R. C. *Interpreting the Gospels*. Nashville: Abingdon Press, 1973. pp. 59-137.

Hamann, H. P. *A Popular Guide to New Testament Criticism*. St. Louis: Concordia Publishing House, 1979.

Harrison, Waltke, Guthrie, Fee. *Biblical Criticism*. Grand Rapids: Zondervan Publishing Corporation, 1978.

Hoyer, T. *The Story of the Church*. St. Louis: Concordia Publishing House, 1942. Chapters 6-7, pp. 89-115.

Kistemaker, S. *The Gospels in Current Study*. Grand Rapids: Baker Book House, 1972. pp. 27-61.

Krentz, E. *Biblical Studies Today*. St. Louis: Concordia Publishing House, 1966. pp. 13-40.

Ladd, G. E. *The New Testament and Criticism*. Grand Rapids: William B. Eerdmans Publishing Co., 1974.

Linneman, Eta. *Historical Criticism of the Bible*. Grand Rapids: Baker Book House, 1990.

Martin, R. *New Testament Foundations*. Grand Rapids: Zondervan Publishing Corporation, 1971.

Marshall, I. H. *New Testament Interpretation*. Grand Rapids: William B. Eerdmans Publishing Co., 1977.

McKnight, E. *What is Form Criticism?* Philadelphia: Fortress Press, 1969.

Mitton, C. Jesus: *The Fact Behind the Faith*. Grand Rapids: William B. Eerdmans Publishing Co., 1974.

Perrin, N. *What is Redaction Criticism?* Philadelphia: Fortress Press, 1969.

Roth, R. *Story and Reality*. Grand Rapids: William B. Eerdmans Publishing Co., 1973.

Stein, R. H. *The Synoptic Problem*. Grand Rapids: Baker Book House, 1987.

_____ . *Gospels and Tradition: Studies on Redaction Criticism of the Synoptic Gospels*. Grand Rapids: Baker Book House, 1991.

Part Three

THREE
HISTORICAL-CRITICAL
METHODS
OF INTERPRETATION

10

EXISTENTIAL DEMYTHOLOGIZING—
BULTMANN'S APPROACH

The men who practiced rationalistic criticism in the last half of the 19th century cast a shadow of doubt over the content of any book of the Bible on which they practiced their "art." In the 1920s, however, a new Lutheran "champion" rose to "rescue Christianity" from the loss of most of the Bible. Rudolph Bultmann, by using existential demythologizing as the way to interpret the words of the Bible, supposedly enabled Christians to hold on to the New Testament as the "Word of God" without giving up the "scientific" insights of rationalistic literary criticism.

We could choose to use any one of many theologians to illustrate this form of the historical-critical method, but Bultmann seems to be the most logical. Interpreters in the radical spectrum of the historical-critical method are measured most often by the degree to which they follow Bultmann's approach. It was his essay *New Testament and Mythology* that started a discussion that led to a whole new method of New Testament interpretation, which was adopted by many church leaders including Roman Catholic, Lutheran (ELCA), and Reformed.

The New Hermeneutic

In the process of this new method of interpretation called *Hermeneutic,* Bible interpretation was widened from "mere interpretation" of the words of Scripture to an "understanding of the whole human existence." To pursue the deciphering of what the texts of the New Testament books had to say to an ancient group of unknown readers who lived in a nonscientific world was dismissed by Bultmann as idle curiosity. However, to make sense of these texts, to interpret them in terms of human existence for modern man—this is considered to be the true work of the interpreter.

THE DEEPER MEANING

The understanding of human existence

The first step in the New Hermeneutic is to use the insights of rationalistic literary criticism to determine where a passage fits in the strata of the New Testament material. Simply put, when did a given verse or set of verses originate? Is it a fact, or was it something that developed in the oral tradition, the literary sources, or the redaction process. Once one has identified what kind of material he is reading, the second step is to interpret all this material from the perspective of existential demythologizing. In this way a person will supposedly be confronted with the *kerygma* of the text.

Kerygma

The key to understanding the New Testament according to Bultmann is the realization that its message is not actual history but the *kerygma* of the early church. *Kerygma* is a Greek word that means "preaching."

Ernst Kaesemann, a disciple of Bultmann, explains: "The early church wrote primarily as reportage and in its kerygma overlays and conceals the figure of the historical Jesus . . . It interprets out of its existence what for it has already become mere history and employs for this purpose the medium of its preaching. It is precisely by this method . . . [that it] rescues the facts of the past from being regarded only as prodigies and wonders . . . and allows the historical events . . . to pass into oblivion . . . and replaces them by its own message."[1]

Kerygma, then, is the "preaching" of the people of the New Testament time whose real message is not the seemingly historical events it reports about Jesus. Rather, its real message is the interpretation of human existence that is couched in the non-scientific expressions of the early church.

An example of kerygma would be an explanation, such as the following, of Jesus' stilling of the storm (Mark 4): This miracle never happened. It is a "story" that contains a deeper meaning. It tells people today that they can find peace in the storms of life swirling around them. In this way this "parable" becomes a modern event in which the "word" has a powerful meaning for everyone.

It is apparent from this example that kerygma is really nothing but a new form of allegorizing. The basic fault of allegorizing is that it permits the interpreter to skip over what the words of Scripture say objectively and substitute what he subjectively determines they really mean. Note how this happens in kerygma: the objective meaning of the words is replaced by their existential meaning, which is determined subjectively by the modern day reader as he searches the text for a message about his true being.

KERYGMA

(a new form of allegorizing)

[Means¹ = History]

Means² = Human Existence

But Bultmann went further than to deny that this kerygma or "preaching" of the early church was history. He also said that it has no objective meaning apart from its meaning at the time it is read or proclaimed. Note the existential overtone that only the present is a reality.

The subjective nature of kerygma is not considered a weakness by Bultmann. Rather, it is proclaimed as its real strength. Kerygma, he insists, is what sets the New Testament apart from any other book and makes it unique. Kerygma is the special form of theological statement in which God chooses to encounter each individual by means of the existential message contained in these words.

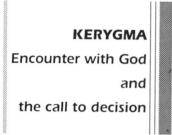

KERYGMA

Encounter with God

and

the call to decision

In this encounter, God calls on the individual to make a decision. This decision is a momentous one because it requires a total change in one's attitude and in the way one lives. Kerygma is thus also a unique kind of language, a mythical language, in which God meets man in the form of words.

Mythical language

Bultmann felt that taking the words of the New Testament literally would be putting an unnecessary stumbling block *(skandalon)* in the road that the unbeliever must travel to become a believer. When a literal reading of the words presents a supernatural idea (e.g., Christ is both divine and human) or event (e.g., changing water into wine) to the mind of the modern reader, this becomes a stumbling block. He called anything that involved the supernatural in any way a "false skandalon" because it represented an ancient worldview that he said is no longer acceptable today.

People at Jesus' time believed that world events as well as events in their own personal lives were influenced by gods, angels, and devils. We know in our modern scientific world, Bultmann said, that we live in a closed world with a roof over us, through which no gods or angels can reach down to influence our lives, and a floor under us, through which no devils can reach up to influence our lives.

In his essay *Jesus Christ and Mythology* Bultmann wrote,

MYTH

Picture Language:

theological truth

in story form

"The worldview of Scripture is mythological and . . . unacceptable to modern man whose thinking is shaped by science . . . Have you read anywhere in newspapers that political or social or economic events are performed by supernatural powers such as gods, angels or demons?"[2]

This "false skandalon" of the supernatural is removed by recognizing that the New Testament kerygma is couched in mythical language. "Myth" is a special kind of truth. It is picture language that expresses the theological significance of certain events or realities in story form. For example, the truth that in Jesus we can be changed from living a useless life into living a useful life is pictured by the story of Jesus changing water into wine.

But considering the language of the New Testament mythological does not remove every skandalon. It supposedly removes the "false skandalon" because a person no longer has to sacrifice his intellect in order to accept a view of the world that he denies in his everyday life. The "true skandalon" still remains because the New Testament kerygma with its mythical language challenges a person to make the decision to enter an authentic kind of human existence. Only the Bible has this kind of language and only the Bible presents the "true skandalon" to its readers. This is Bultmann's version of the basic principle of interpretation, *sola Scriptura* (by Scripture alone).

Before a person is confronted by the true skandalon, however, this mythical language must be "demythologized" by him or for him. Only demythologized words will make him aware that God is challenging him to find his true being. The key to demythologizing or unlocking the meaning of the mythological language of the New Testament is found, Bultmann insisted, in existential philosophy.

The role of existential philosophy

Some might feel that a handicap is imposed on the ordinary layperson by the New Testament being recorded in mythological language. It might make the Bible a closed book to him if he does not know how to break the code of this special kind of language. But this does not happen, Bultmann argued, because every human being is absorbed in the question of the meaning of his own life. Every person has the basic existential "preunderstanding" which will prompt him to ask the right questions of Scripture.

To begin with, he will ask a very general question: What does Scripture have to say about human existence? When a person addresses this question to Scripture, he in turn will be asked challenging questions by Scripture that will give him a new and deeper insight into his own personal existence. With this new insight he will be able to ask more specific questions of Scripture. In turn he will be challenged by the new questions that Scripture will put to him. This is Bultmann's hermeneutical circle.

Again, let Bultmann speak for himself:

> The method is nothing other than a kind of questioning. . . . I cannot understand a given text without asking certain questions of it. . . . If we must ask the right questions which are concerned with the possibilities of understanding human existence then the proper conceptions by which such understanding is expressed must be taken from philosophy. . . . The philosophy today which offers the conceptions for understanding human existence is directly the object of attention. . . . Existentialist philosophy urges man "You must exist!" Without this decision, without the readiness to be a human being, no one can understand a single word of the Bible which speaks to personal existence. . . . Whether the interpreter can enter into it (what is meant) depends then on how far he is open to the range of what is possible for man. In the end, therefore, the question regarding the possibility of understanding a text depends on what openness the exegete has to the existential possibility as a human possibility, what interpretation the exegete has of himself as a man.[3]

The role of the interpreter

The task of the interpreter is to establish the existential meaning of the kerygma, which is couched in the mythical language of the New Testament. It is a simple task, Bultmann says; all the interpreter has to do is explain what each passage says to man about his authentic being. Several examples from Bultmann's sermons will illustrate how this is done.

The interpreter is to show what the text says to a person about one's authentic being.

In a sermon on the Pharisee and the publican, Bultmann sees the Pharisee as a man who is obsessed with his position in this world, that is, he is very concerned whether he is worth something in the eyes of other people or not. The publican has found freedom and security in the knowledge that he is worth something. He does this, not by comparing himself with other people in the world, but by fleeing from himself and seeking refuge in God. His true self-knowledge, his authentic being, does not come from knowing that others admire him but from knowing he must flee to God's grace if he is to have any value.

Bultmann's summary of the meaning of this text is that the justified man is the man who in true spiritual freedom has lowered his eyes before God and thus become one who has a spirit of sincere, honest, and "self-forgetful" service. The final sentence says, "If our parable persuades anyone to adopt this new way of life, on such a one Jesus has exercised his liberating redemptive power."[4]

In a sermon on the miraculous catch of fish (Luke 5:1-10), Bultmann begins by applying rationalistic literary criticism to the passage. He says about this pericope, "I consider it to be pious fiction . . . a poetic image mirroring the power Jesus exercises over a human life."[5] Next he demythologizes this "poetic image" to find its existential message for the modern reader.

Bultmann felt that since this myth follows on the disciples' toiling all night, it shows that Jesus' wonder-working word will come to a person only when he realizes that his own resources are exhausted. Then Jesus will tell him to put out into the deep and let his net down where he will no longer choose to do what he wants, but he will act at God's command. When he does this, his net will be filled, that is, he will find his authentic being by living a life of love. He will bear witness to what God has done in him by the way he acts toward his fellowmen.

Bultmann's treatment of the wedding of Cana, and the Good Shepherd chapter in John illustrates how much rationalistic literary criticism pervades his Bible interpretation and how similar existential demythologizing is to allegorizing.

In regard to the miracle at the wedding of Cana, he says that there can be little doubt that this story is taken over from heathen legend since it is so typical of the Dionysius legend. The wine stands for both the gift Jesus gives man and for

Jesus himself as the revealer of man's true existence. The water stands for everything that man substitutes for Jesus in his attempt to find his true existence, things such as the treasures and pleasures of the world. These are the things by which man thinks he can find true happiness, but which inevitably fail him when they are put to the test.

Jesus' refusal of Mary's suggestion that he do something to help indicates that God's revelation to us of our true being is independent of human desires. It cannot be forcibly brought about by man's supplication. Rather, it comes to pass where and how God wills, and then it surpasses all human expectation.

In the interpretation of the Good Shepherd chapter, Bultmann first undertakes a rearranging of the material to get the "right slant." He dismisses Jesus' statement that he is the door as a gloss that confuses things. And when Jesus says that he will lay down his life, this is called an interpolation that interrupts and really does not follow at all because the surrender of Jesus' life is his exaltation. Bultmann says: "It is precisely because he [Jesus] is nothing for himself, he has absolute freedom . . . and truly shows himself to be the Revealer." Since John's shepherd speaks of a reciprocal relationship of shepherd and sheep, (Jesus knows his sheep and they hear his voice and follow him), it is supposed to have been taken over from the Gnostic tradition. Bultmann says that John jettisons much of the Gnostic element but retains the idea "that man's true being is more than his temporal existence. . . . Man (the sheep) has from the very beginning a relationship to the Revealer . . . and everyone has the possibility of discovering his true being in belonging to the Revealer."[6]

One final example from Bultmann is his explanation of the raising of Lazarus. It illustrates how death is understood in existential demythologizing. Bultmann says that Jesus "corrects" Martha's idea of a future resurrection by raising Lazarus immediately. This myth, therefore, stresses that there is only one resurrection for the believer, a present resurrection, which is grasped by faith.

The New Testament expressions of human death and resurrection are only images and hints. One may suffer the earthly death, but, Bultmann says, this cannot disturb the "life" which the man who finds his true being has in a higher ultimate sense. Thus death to one who has found his true being is unreal. "Do you believe this?" Jesus asks Martha. Bultmann suggests that by this question Jesus is asking whether man is ready to let life and death, as he has known them, be unreal. Martha's answer shows that she recognizes that in Jesus the eschatological invasion of God into the world has taken place.

The Christ event

As the interpreter demythologizes a text in this way and explains the existential meaning of the text for people, the "Christ event" (also called the "eschatological event") can take place. In this "event" God encounters a person in the existential message of a given passage. In this encounter God challenges the person to be what he is meant to be (authentic being). The person then has to make the decision whether to accept God's challenge or not.

If a person makes the decision (which Bultmann calls "faith") in this encounter with God to be what he is meant to be, then God will lead him to make the cross of Christ his

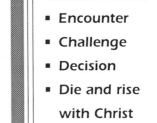

CHRIST EVENT

- **Encounter**
- **Challenge**
- **Decision**
- **Die and rise**
  with Christ

own. He will die with Christ, that is, he will deny the ever present temptation of trying to allay his anxiety (his "flesh") by surrendering himself to the world and immersing himself in its being (the "law"). This is the negative side of his eschatological or Christ event (finding his true being).

The positive side of the "Christ event" is that while God is leading a person to make the cross of Christ his own, God is also leading him to participate in Jesus' resurrection (also called the "Easter event"). He will rise with Christ, that is, he will begin the process of finding the freedom (the "gospel") to be his own true self (his "spirit"). He will gradually become more and more open to God's love and will live in unselfish love toward others. That the "Easter event" has begun to take place in his life will also be evident by his complete lack of concern for the possessions and the pleasures of the world as well as by a nonchalance about the future. Note that the "Christ event" does not take place suddenly, in a momentary flash of insight. It is often instead a lengthy process in which, as a person grows in faith, he becomes more and more the kind, loving person God wants him to be.

Bultmann writes: "Jesus' word invites man to decide for the reign of God breaking in. . . . Do men really want God's reign? Or is it the world they want? The decision they must make is a radical one . . . to abandon all earthly ties . . . to turn away from himself and place himself at the disposal of others."[7]

The historical Jesus

Because the New Testament is said to be couched in mythical language, the point is argued whether the historical Jesus is important or not. Bultmann felt that the "quest for the historical Jesus" must be abandoned since faith does not rest on the knowledge of some person from the past. It is not important to establish any historical facts about Jesus. It is important only that one decides to be what God wants him to be as Jesus did. The Christian's faith, Bultmann said, rests only on his being renewed again and again in his personal "Christ event." This takes place only as a person listens to the kerygmatic call to decision as it is voiced in the kerygma of the early Christian church.

Bultmann even says that it is a sure sign of "unfaith" to seek support for faith in historical facts about Jesus. The message of Jesus, he insists, is a presupposition for the theology of the New Testament rather than a part of that theology itself.

Some of Bultmann's disciples—Fuchs, Ebeling, Kaesemann—are considered to be the leading spokesmen of existential demythologizing in the world today. These men argue that the historical Jesus must not be entirely ignored lest faith become only a faith in the early church. They admit that to establish facts about Jesus is a difficult process because of the strata of biblical material. But they also firmly believe that the knowledge that some facts and sayings of Jesus are genuine should spur the scholar on.

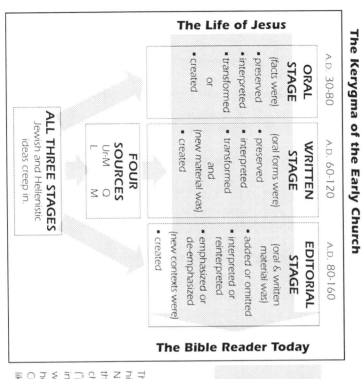

EXISTENTIAL DEMYTHOLOGIZING

DEMYTHOLOGIZE the KERYGMA to find the message about HUMAN EXISTENCE

"THE CHRIST EVENT" ("die" and "rise" with Christ)

This chart shows how the most radical approach of the historical-critical method views the interpretation of the New Testament. It accepts rationalistic literary criticism (the three stages of development in the kerygma of the early church) as fact. Anything supernatural in this kerygma ("preaching") of the early church is a myth that must be interpreted existentially (existential demythologizing). In this way the reader is challenged to find his "true existence." If he takes the challenge ("faith"), he will gradually die like Christ did to the material things of life and gradually rise like Christ did to live a life of love ("Christ event").

Scholars who follow this approach to Bible interpretation may vary in their opinions as to what is historical, but they agree that all sincere searching for facts about Jesus and the resulting propositions ought not be ignored. Careful panning for flakes of gold from the original vein of history must be done. These flakes will be hard to find, they admit, because they are concealed in the kerygma by the interpretation, transformation, and creation done by the early church. But any kind of discovery of any original material, no matter how little, is worth the effort, they say.

Summary

The radical historical-critical method of Bultmann accepts rationalistic literary criticism and uses it fully. At the same time, it attempts to avoid the loss of any part of the New Testament for the modern reader by saying that the New Testament is a new kind of language, mythological language. Understanding this language requires that it be demythologized since it is the kerygma of the nonscientific people of the early church. At the same time, this approach says that the New Testament has a new purpose, an existential purpose. Discovering this new purpose requires that the reader approach the text with the willingness to find his true existence in his Christ event. The diagram on the previous page gives an overview of the process involved in this example of one of the approaches used by those who practice the historical-critical method of interpretation.

NOTES

1. Ernst Kaesemann, *Essays on New Testament Themes* (Naperville, IL: Allenson, 1964), pp. 19,20.

2. Rudolph Bultmann, *Jesus Christ and Mythology* (New York: Charles Scribner's Sons, 1958), pp. 36,37.

3. *Ibid.,* pp. 49ff.

4. Rudolph Bultmann, *This World and the Beyond* (New York: Charles Scribner's Sons, 1960), p. 133.

5. *Ibid.,* p. 158.

6. Rudolph Bultmann, *The Gospel of John* (Philadelphia: Westminster Press, 1971), p. 374.

7. Rudolph Bultmann, *Primitive Christianity in Its Contemporary Setting* (New York: Meridian Books, 1956), pp. 90,92.

BIBLIOGRAPHY—CHAPTER TEN

Achtemeier, P. *An Introduction to the New Hermeneutic.* Philadelphia: Westminster Press, 1969.

Anderson, C. *The Historical Jesus: A Continuing Quest.* Grand Rapids: William B. Eerdmans Publishing Co., 1972.

Bultmann, R. *Existence and Faith.* New York: Meridian Books, 1960.

_____ . *The Gospel of St. John.* Philadelphia: Westminster Press, 1971.

_____ . *Jesus Christ and Mythology.* New York: Charles Scribner's Sons, 1958.

_____ . *Kerygma and Mythology.* New York: Harper and Row, 1961.

_____ . *Primitive Christianity in Its Contemporary Setting.* New York: Meridian Books, 1956.

_____ . *This World and the Beyond.* New York: Charles Scribner's Sons, 1960.

Ebeling, G. *The Problem of Historicity in the Church and Its Proclamation.* Philadelphia: Fortress Press, 1967.

_____ . *Word and Faith.* Philadelphia: Fortress Press, 1963.

Fuchs, E. *Studies of the Historical Jesus.* Naperville, IL: Allenson, 1964.

Henderson, I. *Myth in the New Testament.* Chicago: Regnery Publishing, Inc., 1952.

_____ . *Rudolph Bultmann.* Richmond: John Knox Press, 1952.

Henry, C. F. *Frontiers in Modern Theology.* Chicago: Moody Press, 1965.

Kaehler, M. *The So-called Historical Jesus and the Historic Biblical Christ.* Philadelphia: Fortress Press, 1964.

Kaesemann, E. *Essays on New Testament Themes.* Naperville, IL: Allenson, 1964.

Kegley, C. (ed.). *The Theology of Rudolf Bultmann.* New York: Harper and Row, 1966.

Kistemaker, S. *Interpreting God's Word Today.* Grand Rapids: Baker Book House, 1970.

Klooster, F. *Quests for the Historical Jesus.* Grand Rapids: Baker Book House, 1977.

Kuemmel, W. *The New Testament: The History of the Investigation of Its Problems.* Nashville: Abingdon Press, 1972.

_____ . *Introduction to the New Testament.* Nashville: Abingdon Press, 1966.

Lindsell, H. *The Battle for the Bible.* Grand Rapids: Zondervan Publishing Corporation, 1976.

Montgomery, J. W. *Myth, Allegory, and Gospel.* Minneapolis: Bethany House, 1974.

Nash, R. *Christian Faith and Historical Understanding.* Grand Rapids: Zondervan Publishing Corporation, 1984.

Robinson, J. A. T. *Can We Trust the New Testament?* Grand Rapids: William B. Eerdmans Publishing Co., 1977.

Pinnock, C. H. *Biblical Revelation.* Chicago: Moody Press, 1971.

Smart, J. D. *The Strange Silence of the Bible in the Church.* Philadelphia: Westminster Press, 1970.

11

GOSPEL REDUCTIONISM

Background

Bultmann's existential demythologizing became common-place in the liberal Lutheran bodies in the United States that now belong to the Evangelical Lutheran Church in America (ELCA). This form of the historical-critical method was too radical for a more conservative church body such as the Lutheran Church—Missouri Synod.

However, some in the Missouri Synod felt that they could incorporate some aspects of the historical-critical method into the interpretation of the Bible and still retain Lutheran doctrine. The approach they adopted was to say that the divine part of the New Testament was limited to passages that contained the message of the gospel. Thus this approach is often referred to as "gospel reductionism." The rest of Scripture, they said, is human, especially those parts that are primarily historical.

Many of the men who were the leaders of this movement later left

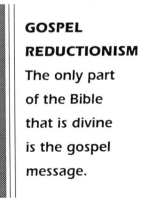

GOSPEL REDUCTIONISM The only part of the Bible that is divine is the gospel message.

the Missouri Synod to join ELCA. However, the great majority of the students whom they trained over several decades and who became pastors and teachers remained. They continue to form a rather large and influential group within this church body at this time.

The men who introduced gospel reductionism in the Missouri Synod faced opposition from the start. As their position became clearer from what these men wrote and taught, the opposition grew. A president of the synod was eventually elected who was determined to address this growing controversy in the synod. That president was Jacob Preus.

In 1972 Preus, as president of the Missouri Synod, asked for and received the report of a fact-finding committee about the new approach to interpretation being promoted at that time by most of the faculty members at the seminary in St. Louis. Subsequently he wrote: "While the principal doctrines of the Christian faith in most instances still appear to be upheld, the stage has been set for an erosion of the very fundamentals . . . Not only does this method of Biblical interpretation introduce the principle of uncertainty into Christian faith and theology, but its underlying assumptions about the nature of Holy Scripture and its authority are so foreign to the Bible, classical Christianity, and the Lutheran Confessions that we must regard it as a false doctrine of Holy Scriptures."[1] It is the essential truth of this analysis which this chapter will illustrate.

In looking at this type of historical-critical interpretation, this chapter will focus on the writings of the men who left Concordia Seminary at St. Louis to form Seminex (Seminary in Exile). By the late 1960s these men formed a large majority of the faculty. One major source for the content of this chapter is the *Concordia Theological Monthly* (CTM) from 1968 to 1973. The CTM was the theological journal for which these men had editorial responsibility. Another source is their position as they enunciated it in a statement titled "Faithful to Our Calling—Faithful to Our Lord."[2]

The basic view

The conclusions of rationalistic literary criticism are accepted as facts in gospel reductionism. For example, the development of the synoptic gospels in three stages—from oral tradition to written sources to the work of redactors—is a basic starting point for the interpreter. However, in gospel reductionism it is said that the Holy Spirit influenced this whole process. Rather than an inspiration of individual writers, it is suggested that there was an inspiration of the Christian community. This does not mean that every word is divinely inspired. Instead, at the same time as the human process was taking place in which the accounts of Jesus' life evolved through the three stages, a divine process also took place. The human accounts of Jesus' life were infused with divine truth by the Holy Spirit. Thus the gospels are at the same time both a human account and a divine word.

The Bible is a HUMAN ACCOUNT into which the Holy Spirit injected DIVINE TRUTH.

The human side of the Bible is considered a legitimate field of investigation for the principles of the rationalistic historian. At the same time, it is said that the divine side of the Bible goes beyond historiographical research and can be investigated and understood only by the believer in whom the Holy Spirit has worked saving faith.

Thus the basic view of the Bible is that a division can be made between its human side and its divine side. For the answer to the question how this division is handled by the person who wants to retain basic Christian doctrine, one has to look at the characteristics of the Bible as they are defined by gospel reductionism.

The characteristics of the Bible

Those who practice gospel reductionism insist that any serious inductive study of the Bible as history will lead to the conclusion that the Bible participates in human weakness and error. References are made, for example, to the "contradictions" in some of the parallel accounts of the gospels. But this characteristic of the Bible, it is argued, should not disturb a believer.

By faith the Christian is supposed to have gained a spiritual perspective which recognizes that the Holy Spirit is able to overcome the error-prone human process from which the New Testament emerged. The Christian expects that through his investigation of the divine side of the Word he will hear God address him in both judgment and mercy. In other words, another characteristic of the Bible is that the Holy Spirit reveals truth in it despite the erroneous historical setting in which this truth appears.

The human part of the Bible is not considered totally accurate. Its statements on history and nature are open to challenge. However, since it is a record compiled by the early church, it nevertheless remains the most important historical evidence for those events to which it witnesses and which it interprets. Any challenge made against its historical accuracy must be carefully investigated and proved before the biblical record can be called erroneous.

The HISTORICAL ACCURACY of the Bible is determined by "scholars."

Despite this seemingly conservative precaution, note how the accuracy of the biblical record has been shifted to a position where it is subject to the decisions of "scholars." Without the "scholars'" help, a person can no longer be sure that what he reads in the Bible about history or nature is literally true.

In this way the unity and inerrancy of Scripture are also called into question. When "scholars" agree that there are "contradictions" in Scripture, no one can maintain that the Bible agrees perfectly in all that it teaches.

INERRANCY means the Bible brings people to faith.

The unity of the Bible is reduced to those passages that speak about God's judgment and mercy. The inerrancy of the Bible is changed in meaning so that it no longer applies to what Scripture says but to what it accomplishes. Inspiration, the gospel reductionist says, means that God sees to it that his Word does what he intends it to do, namely, to bring people to faith. Only in this sense and only in the fulfillment of this function is the Bible spoken of as being inerrant, in perfect agreement, and wholly reliable. Note that the inerrancy of Scripture is really being equated with what is normally referred to as its efficacy.

In gospel reductionism the Bible is viewed as a collection of timeless truths with no real, vital historical connection. Lest this conclusion seem overdrawn, consider this quotation from "Faithful to Our Calling," noting especially the stress on the relative unimportance of the historical dimension of Scripture.

> The historical character of the Scripture means that we cannot demand that the Bible authors possess the same knowledge of science or geology as we do, or that they operate with the same criteria of what is history or accuracy. The reliability or "inerrancy" of the Scriptures cannot be determined by twentieth century standards of factuality. Nor do the Scriptures link the work of the Holy Spirit with this kind of "inerrancy." The purpose of the Spirit imparted by our Lord is to lead us into the whole truth about what God was doing in Jesus Christ, that we might be redeemed and glorified. In disclosing that Truth God does not err, and in achieving that purpose the Spirit active in the Word does not lead us astray; to that the Spirit within us bears witness.[3]

The principles of interpretation

When dealing with the New Testament in its historical dimension, the gospel reductionist applies the same principles that are used to interpret any other literature. Among these are the necessity of using the literary and historical contexts, and the fact that each passage has only one literal sense. Unfortunately, they go beyond this and also include the methodology of rationalistic literary criticism:

> Basically all the techniques associated with historical-critical methodology, such as source analysis, form history, and redaction history, are legitimated by the fact that God chose to use as his written Word human documents written by human beings in human language.[4]

The literary criticism of rationalism is declared "neutral" in how it deals with Scripture.

The fact that source analysis, form history, and redaction history are based on rationalism's denial of the supernatural is ignored, and the historical-critical methodology is declared neutral. It is assumed that if Christian presuppositions are used in employing this methodology, the results will bring great blessing to the church.

The Christian presuppositions listed are: the centrality of the gospel in Scripture, the distinction between Law and Promise, and the Spirit's gift of faith as the necessary prerequisite to understand the Promise and receive it. Notable by its absence is any mention of verbal inspiration. This Christian presupposition is undoubtedly dropped because it is incompatible with rationalistic literary criticism and its denial of the supernatural and also because "scholars" have "proved" that there are "contradictions" in the biblical record.

Other false methods of interpretation that have worked so much havoc in the Christian church at various stages in its history are given a nod of approval. It is said that just as the Holy Spirit worked through the allegorical school of exegesis and the fourfold senses of the medieval exegetes, so also today he works through both the historical-grammatical and the historical-critical methodology.

Why do gospel reductionists ignore the evil of those earlier methods and actually approve them? It makes sense only if one realizes that they want to establish the principle that there is a constant need for change in the way the church interprets Scripture in order to meet the changing settings of the church. They argue that sometimes two contrasting methods can be complementary. As the weakness of one method becomes evident as the church encounters new situations, they believe that the church should gradually abandon or modify that method in order to accommodate new insights.[5]

On the basis of such reasoning, the position is adopted that the interpreter must learn to adapt to the modern setting of the church. He must not begin to read the human side of the New Testament as a statement of fact to be taken at its surface meaning. This, it is argued, just does not fit in with the present-day view of history. Rather, the interpreter must treat the human record as a theological view of the world, of history, and of man that is expressed in terms derived from the ancient culture from which it emerged.

Concentration on the divine message

In spite of the problems faced by the interpreter in working with the human side of Scripture, it was maintained that the true doctrine could be retained by the proper interpretation of its divine side. To do this the interpreter must study the New Testament with the expectation of hearing exclusively law or gospel.

In fact, gospel reductionism condemns the interpreter who insists that the Bible is historically factual. Such an interpreter is said to be leading people away from Christ because he is leading them to accept God's Word on the basis of historical verification rather than by faith alone. His interpretation is labeled a subtle attempt to substitute sight for faith.

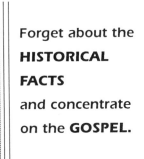

Forget about the **HISTORICAL FACTS** and concentrate on the **GOSPEL.**

Gospel reductionism makes the gospel normative in such a way as to deny the normative authority of the whole Bible. A false antithesis is set up between the gospel and the Bible:

> The Gospel gives the Scriptures their normative character, not vice versa. We are saved by grace through faith in Jesus Christ alone, not through faith in Christ and something else, even if that something else be the Bible itself.[6]

This rejection of Scripture as God's revealed and inerrant Word except for its gospel content has disastrous results. It is an attempt to ride the fence between skepticism and confidence in the reliability of the Bible. Scripture warns us, and history proves, that any attempt to balance skepticism and confidence in regard to God's Word will slowly but surely tip in favor of skepticism. A look at the doctrinal results in gospel reductionism gives us one more example of this axiom.

The doctrinal results

Perhaps the best way to illustrate the results is to look at what gospel reductionism does in the interpretation of the four gospels. The gospels are considered composites of the conflicting traditions of what Jesus meant to the early Christians. Many of Jesus' words and works are considered free adaptations or even contrived stories about what Jesus said and did. For example, an article in the 1972 *Concordia Theological Monthly* titled "Parables in the Gospel of Thomas" allows that the apocryphal gospel of Thomas may have a more primitive, and thus perhaps a more accurate, form of Jesus' parable about the husbandman and the caretakers of the vineyard than is found in Luke's gospel.

> **The "writer's intent" is not determined by what the inspired writer says but by the subjective judgment of the interpreter.**

The standard for determining whether something is historical or not is based on whether the writer intended the passage to be historical or not. At first glance this does not sound too bad. Obviously, if the writer intended what he wrote to be understood figuratively instead of historically, that is the way we should interpret it. But a closer look at what the gospel reductionist means reveals that the "writer's intent" is not to be determined objectively from the writer's own words. Rather, it is something that the modern interpreter may determine subjectively according to his own judgment.

The result is that there are divergent views about the historical nature of the words and works of Jesus recorded in the gospels. The general view is that Jesus' words and miracles are possibly historical but not necessarily so. This vague position allows for varying opinions.

On the one hand, there are those who think that few, if any, of the events recorded in the gospels are historical. They do not deny that God could have inspired the early Christian community to retain some of Jesus' actual words. They just don't think God did this. They also say the same thing about Jesus' miracles. They do not deny the supernatural, and therefore they do not deny that miracles could have happened. They just do not think that they did.

On the other hand, there are those who believe that most, if not all, of the words and works of Jesus are historical. But they believe that it is not necessary for the retention of the gospel that this view of the historical nature of the gospel record be accepted by their doubting colleagues. Thus, those who deny the words and miracles of Jesus are willing to grant the possibility that they might be historical, while those who accept Jesus' words and miracles as historical are willing to grant that they possibly might not be historical.

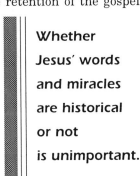

Whether Jesus' words and miracles are historical or not is unimportant.

This agreement to disagree doesn't bother the gospel reductionist because he insists that "to edify the Church, we ought to focus on the central meaning of the miracle accounts for us instead of dwelling on the authenticity of isolated miraculous details."[7] In the miracle of the feeding of the 5,000, for example, whether 5,000 or 2,000 people were fed or whether this was done 1,000 or 2,000 years ago is not of major importance. The important thing is the truth that this parable teaches, namely, that God in love provides for our bodily needs.

The parable of the good Samaritan and the parable of the rich man and Lazarus are cited as illustrations of how spiritual truths can be conveyed even though the events themselves may or may not be historical. We do not know whether the good Samaritan or the rich man and Lazarus were actual people or just people made up by Jesus. Yet we believe and apply to ourselves the truths that Jesus teaches us in these stories. That is the way the whole New Testament should be handled, it is argued. Then historical discrepancies will not invalidate passages as God's Word, because faith will rest on God's ability to teach us what he wishes by these words rather than resting on the accuracy of the historians of an ancient culture.

Faith concerns itself with the LESSON TAUGHT rather than with the HISTORICAL ACCURACY of an account.

This approach is then also applied to a miracle that is an essential part of the gospel account—the resurrection. It is said that there are contradictions in this account but this really doesn't make any difference. The circumstances of Jesus' resurrection and the fact of his resurrection are matters of lesser importance. The only thing of real importance in this account is the truth that Jesus completed our salvation.

To handle Scripture interpretation this way is to ignore one simple fact that is fundamental to proper interpretation. It is absolutely wrong to say that what Scripture presents as parables and what Scripture presents as historical events are to be interpreted in the same way. The gospel reductionist does this only because he has set himself up as the judge of what is and what is not historical in the Scripture.

The gospel is watered down to the "Promise"

While one's first reaction might be relief that at least the gospel is being maintained, even this relief is short-lived when it becomes apparent that there is a lack of clarity as to just what the gospel is. Often the fruits of faith, such as good works or social action, are equated with the gospel. In an approach that is concerned with nothing in the Bible except the gospel, confusion about the meaning of the gospel can be the final step by which Satan robs its adherents of the truth.

It became evident in two ways that there was a noticeable drift in gospel reductionism away from the message of Scripture centering in Jesus' redeeming work toward a vague understanding of the gospel. One is the definition of the gospel given in "Faithful to Our Calling." The other surfaces in the writings of various men in the *Concordia Theological Monthly*.

In "Faithful to Our Calling" this statement is made about the gospel:

> In the last analysis, the gospel message is for each of us. God declares that through the life, death, and resurrection of Jesus Christ he has acted in the past on our behalf, and now promises to free us from any force that enslaves us.[8]

The last part of this statement is so vague that it could serve as a definition of the gospel for almost anyone who believes in some kind of benevolent God. The gospel is often referred to as "the promise." The effect of the Promise is defined as a believer's confidence that God is at work in human history to bring blessings to the family of men.

The PROMISE is defined as the confidence that God is at work for our good.

A contrast is also made between the historical events by which God accomplished our salvation and what God says he did in those events. This contrast seems like only a slight shift, but it is a dangerous one because it tries to separate two things that cannot be separated. If historical events such as Jesus' virgin birth, his death as the God-man, and his resurrection are the very means by which God accomplished our salvation, then any doubt cast on the historicity of those events also undermines our confidence that we are saved. For example, the Bible says that what Jesus' resurrection means for us is completely lost if his resurrection is not a historical fact:

> And if Christ has not been raised, our preaching is useless and so is your faith. . . . And if Christ has not been raised, your faith is futile; you are still in your sins. Then those also who have fallen asleep in Christ are lost. If only for this life we have hope in Christ, we are to be pitied more than all men. (1 Corinthians 15:14,17-19)

Several quotations from the *Concordia Theological Monthly* illustrate further the unclarity about Scripture's message of salvation to which gospel reductionism inevitably leads. Note how the following quotation mistakenly makes love among mankind, which is a fruit of faith, the essence of Christ's redeeming work:

> So God gave us Christ who is, as the writer to the Hebrews says, "the express image of the Father," meaning that God's oneness is in him, that perfect fellowship which God has within himself and with all men. Why else does the Lord become flesh and die and rise from death, except that God by these acts wants to resolve the broken fragmented life of man, to remove hostility, to reestablish fellowship and community.[9]

Note in the next quotation that any clear mention of God's gracious forgiveness of sin is significant by its absence and is replaced by a vague reference to God's love:

> How in all God's world are we to be imitators of our Lord? What in all the heaven is God like? The answer to both questions is the same. Look at Jesus Christ! Jesus Christ is more than the carbon copy of God. He is! He is God made flesh for us. His whole life was a making visible to us the invisible things of God. But more—the purpose of His perfect loving was to create copies of His love on this earth, a real creating again, something out of nothing. He did this by the magnetism of his love. He gave Himself for us—that much He loves—a fragrant offering and sacrifice to God. His life was God's love offered up for us, drawing us to Him as He was lifted up on the cross, a sacrifice. Fragrant—well pleasing—He did not come crabbing, crying, and complaining, but committed to love the Father and to loving us. By His offering He changes us so that we can offer what He did, our lives and our love.[10]

In the final quotation, note how the real meaning of the Lord's Supper is beclouded, if not completely lost:

> We go to the altar to receive the gifts of God in order that we may be able to offer ourselves to Him. We go to the altar of God to offer our public praise and thanksgiving for gifts received. We go to the altar of God so that we might there be empowered to share as God shares, to give as He gives, so that we might be available to others as He is to us.[11]

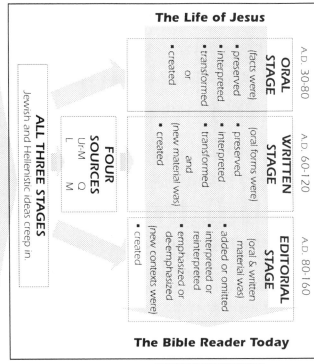

GOSPEL REDUCTIONISM

The Life of Jesus

Human Words

	ORAL STAGE A.D. 30-80	WRITTEN STAGE A.D. 60-120	EDITORIAL STAGE A.D. 80-160
	(facts were) • preserved • interpreted • transformed or • created	(oral forms were) • preserved • interpreted • transformed and (new material was) • created	(oral & written material was) • added or omitted • interpreted or reinterpreted • emphasized or de-emphasized (new contexts were) • created

FOUR SOURCES
Ur-M Q
L M

ALL THREE STAGES
Jewish and Hellenistic ideas creep in.

The Bible Reader Today

Divine Message (Gospel) Injected by the Holy Spirit

A MIXTURE OF DIVINE AND HUMAN CONTENT

This chart shows how another approach of the historical-critical method views the interpretation of the New Testament. It accepts rationalistic literary criticism (the three stages of development in the kerygma of the early church) as the explanation of the development of part of the New Testament record, namely, the human part. This part of the New Testament may contain errors since these are human words. The Holy Spirit injected the truth of the gospel into these human words. Thus the New Testament is a combination of human and divine content. The interpreter needs to distinguish the divine from the human, and can do so by identifying that part of a passage that is a law/gospel message.

207

All of these quotations, it might be argued, could be understood correctly. However, when these quotations are read in context and when one remembers that they come from the pens of men who define the gospel as a vague promise that God is at work for our good, then it becomes apparent that they reflect a view of the Bible that is unacceptable. There is a studied attempt to speak of the gospel in as nebulous terms as possible so that the writer's definition of the gospel will not be a problem for someone else whose view of the gospel is a bit different.

Summary

Gospel reductionism is an attempt to use the historical-critical method without ending up with Bultmann's existential gospel. The diagram on the previous page gives an overview of the process followed by those who use this approach. The New Testament is described as a book with two sides: a divine side and a human side. This division allows a good deal of subjectivity in the interpretation of the Bible. Where the line is to be drawn between the divine and human sides of Scripture becomes a matter of personal choice.

This subjective shrinking of what is divine in the New Testament slowly but surely led to a beclouding of the true understanding of the gospel. Thus the gospel, the one thing that is supposed to be the divine side of the Bible, became a victim of the very method that was to sustain it. President Preus' analysis was correct: While the principal doctrines of the Christian faith appear to be upheld by this method, it really sets the stage for their complete erosion.

Any process of interpretation similar to gospel reductionism is bound to be fatally flawed because any attempt to ride the fence between confidence and skepticism in regard to the words of Scripture will eventually tip more and more in the direction of skepticism.

NOTES

1. Herman Otten, ed., *A Christian Handbook on Vital Issues* (New Haven, MO: Leader Publishing Co., Inc., 1973), pp. 821-826.

2. *Ibid.,* p. 802.

3. *Ibid.,* p. 826.

4. *Ibid.,* p. 826.

5. *Ibid.,* p. 826.

6. *Ibid.,* p. 826.

7. *Ibid.,* p. 823.

8. *Ibid.,* p. 824.

9. *Concordia Theological Monthly,* 1970, p. 511.

10. *Concordia Theological Monthly,* 1969, p. 766.

11. *Concordia Theological Monthly,* 1970, p. 49.

ADDITIONAL READING

1. To get a firsthand impression of gospel reductionism as it was advocated by the professors at Seminex, read their statement "Faithful to Our Calling—Faithful to Our Lord," especially discussions 3,4,5,8, and 9. This statement can be found in *A Christian Handbook on Vital Issues* (New Haven, MO: Leader Publishing Co., Inc., 1973), pp. 821ff.

2. H. Lindsell, *The Battle for the Bible* (Grand Rapids: Zondervan Publishing Corporation), pp. 72-87.

BIBLIOGRAPHY—CHAPTER ELEVEN

Hamann, H. P. *A Popular Guide to New Testament Criticism.* St. Louis: Concordia Publishing House, 1977.

Krentz, E. *Biblical Studies Today.* St. Louis: Concordia Publishing House, 1966.

_____ . *The Historical-Critical Method.* St. Louis: Concordia Publishing House, 1975.

Maier, W. *Form Criticism Reexamined.* St. Louis: Concordia Publishing House, 1973.

Mayer, H. *Interpreting The Holy Scriptures.* St. Louis: Concordia Publishing House, 1967.

Otten, Herman (ed.). *A Christian Handbook on Vital Issues.* New Haven, MO: Leader Publishing Co., Inc., 1973. "Faithful to Our Calling—Faithful to Our Lord," pp. 821ff.

Three pamphlets published by Concordia Publishing House:

Comparative Study of Varying Contemporary Approaches to Biblical Interpretation

Gospel and Scripture

A Lutheran Stance Toward Contemporary Biblical Studies

12

THE DIVINE-HUMAN
MYSTERY APPROACH

We will now examine still another approach to Bible interpretation that is unsatisfactory even though it has been hailed
by some as a conservative view of infallibility and inspiration.
This approach draws heavily on the mystery of the union of
the two natures in Christ.

It is said that, just as this union
of two natures in Christ is impene-
trable by reason and received only
by faith, so it is with the "mystery"
of the human and the divine in the
nature of the Scriptures. The basic
argument is this: Just as one is not
able to resolve all the problems that
the union of the two natures in
Christ may pose for human reason,
so one ought not to expect that he
will be able to solve the problems
that the union of the human and
divine in Scripture poses for human
reason.

**The combination
of the human
and divine
in the Bible
is a mystery
just like
the dual nature
of Christ.**

As in the methods that were discussed in the two previous
chapters, there are also a number of examples of this

approach. The one we will focus on is the form in which it was presented by Harry Boer, a Dutch Reformed author.[1] What Boer says—and this is fairly common among all who use this approach—is that one does not worry about all the inadequacies of human expression such as disparities, gaps, inconsistencies, clashing data, contradictory phenomena, and discrepancies that are evident in the literary, cultural, numerical, or geographical details of Scripture. Faith simply lets these "vicissitudes," or inconsistencies, in Scripture (which are common to all human writing) stand side by side with the Holy Spirit's inspiration of Scripture (which is divine in nature) without attempting any harmonizations that may be contrived to satisfy human reason.

Higher criticism and textual criticism

Boer begins by arguing that rationalistic literary criticism is not to be excluded from the study of the Bible. As a technical academic exercise he believes that higher criticism is as neutral as lower criticism (i.e., textual criticism).

This conclusion of Boer's is based on his faulty analysis of textual criticism. He says it is a science that uses rational, systematic methods and so sets the scholar who practices it "above the divine revelation given in Scripture as its analyst and critic."

Two things are faulty in this analysis. One is that Boer does not give enough emphasis to his own observation that the judgments made in textual criticism are far more objective than those of higher criticism. This, he says in passing, is a "functional" difference, not a formal difference. The fact is that textual criticism has a great deal of objective data, namely, more than 5,300 witnesses to the New Testament text (i.e., papyri, uncials, minuscules, lectionaries, translations, and quotations by church fathers). In higher criticism the data is almost entirely based on subjective conclusions.

For the past century a textual theory based on "intrinsic probability" was built on such subjective theories as recensions and genealogical families of texts. This matter was treated earlier in this book in chapter 7. One family was supposed to be the most reliable, a second family a very loose text, and a third family a late and corrupt text. But this subjective theory has crumbled because of the objective facts presented by the witnesses of the New Testament text, especially the papyri and the versions. Boer is wrong when he says that the difference between higher criticism and textual criticism is functional and not formal.

The second flaw in Boer's equating higher criticism with textual criticism is that the two simply do not deal with the same thing. Textual criticism deals with how certain passages were read differently in various areas of the early church. Higher criticism deals with how the text itself came into being and with how the words are to be interpreted.

Rationalistic textual critics have tried to harmonize the objective facts of textual criticism with their subjective views of the nature of Scripture. But, as was just noted, their theory has been discredited. This will not prevent them from trying again. But Boer's use of their approach to draw the conclusion that textual criticism and higher criticism are similar is not valid.

TEXTUAL CRITICISM deals only with variants that came into the text by hand copying for over 15 centuries.

HIGHER CRITICISM deals with how the text came into being and how it is to be interpreted.

The divine garbed in the human

However, Boer's main point is not to prove that textual criticism and higher criticism are exactly alike. Rather, his aim is to try to prove to Christians that the Bible is a human product as well as a divine product. It is particularly in this way that Boer tries to establish the historical-critical method and its form of literary criticism as a science that has rendered a service to the Christian church.

Boer argues that the human nature of Scripture is being lost by an overemphasis on its divine nature. Higher criticism, he says, has called our attention again to the human side of the Bible by pointing out its inconsistencies, its gaps, its clashing data, and its contradictions. It has had the effect of making Christians realize once again that the "Bible is not only the Book among the many books but also a book among the many books."[2] He welcomes this realization of the Bible's "incarnation in a book" as an antidote to fundamentalism's tendency to view as suspicious and even heretical any statement that the Bible is a human book as well as being divine.

It is at this point that Boer introduces the thought that the Bible is as fully and truly a human book as Christ was fully and truly a human being. He cites some of the "differences" in some passages in the synoptic gospels as proof of this fact: the differences in John the Baptist's words about Jesus being mightier than he; the healing of the blind man while leaving or entering Jericho; the request of James and John made in person or through their mother to Jesus.

> **The fact that the Bible is inspired by the Holy Spirit does not mean it is without clashing data, inconsistencies, and contradictions.**

The differences in these passages, he says, illustrate the divine and human blend in the synoptic gospels. They show that the beauty of the Word of God is dressed in the literary garment of man. They also show that both the writer and the writing were mediated by his mind and heart and will remain fully human in the process of inspiration. These passages demonstrate that just as the humanity of Christ both hides and reveals the divine nature that found embodiment in him, so the humanity of Scripture both hides and reveals the divine reality that is embodied in the Bible. Thus in one sense the Bible cannot be said to be infallible or inerrant since these passages with differences show that the definition of the infallibility of Scripture cannot include the thought that Scripture is without contradictions.

Accommodation to error

The fundamentalist, Boer says, will minimize these passages with differences or will try to harmonize the passages involved. This is done to escape the fact that the critics have punctured the fundamentalist's balloon, which is overblown with a "docetic" view of the nature of Scripture. In this way, he says, the fundamentalist tries to strong-arm the differences in the text by forcing on them a harmonistic exegesis (explanation of a text) demanded by a dogmatic notion of the perfect unity of the Bible. Boer suggests that something else should be done rather than trying to make Scripture perfect as we want it to be, or as we were taught somewhere along the line that it has to be because God is perfect. The solution is to accept the humanity of Scripture as a fact. To illustrate how the humanity veils the divinity of the Bible, he points to the analogy that he says is found in the union of the human with the divine in Christ.

"It is hardly correct to say that Jesus in the days of his flesh was omniscient,"[3] Boer insists. As the Son of God, Jesus had the power of omniscience, but as a man his knowledge was limited. And Boer adds, "Closely related to this limitation is the fact that Jesus again and again accommodated himself to existing beliefs" that we no longer accept in the same form or that are open to question today. As examples Boer cites Jesus' accommodation to the popular belief that sheol (the abode of the dead) has two adjoining divisions, gehenna (hell) and paradise (heaven), and to the belief that Moses wrote the Pentateuch and that Isaiah wrote all of Isaiah. Where Boer is in error in this assumption will be taken up later in this chapter.

In the same way that Jesus accommodated to error, Boer argues, God accommodated to error in Scripture. It is impossible to say that Scripture, which is written by human beings, is absolutely true and in complete harmony. Inspiration does not deprive the scriptural writings of their normal human charac-

> **Inspiration does not mean that the writers lost their human quality of being prone to make errors.**

ter of being subject in all respects to the laws governing the writer's psychical, moral, spiritual, and rational faculties.

The infallibility of Scripture

We cannot deal with the events recorded in Scripture simply as they are recorded, Boer continues. Instead, we must deal with the events as they are interpreted by the writers. A gap exists between the way the writers' contemporaries read what they wrote and the manner in which we, after the passing of 19 centuries, can understand them. The span of time has tended to make us less aware than Jesus' contemporaries of his humanity. This span has also made us less aware than the Christians of the first century of the human quality of the scriptural writers. The task, Boer concludes, "is to ascertain not how inspiration annuls this human quality of the writers, but how it uses it."[4]

> **The infallibility of the Bible should be defined by words such as reliable or trustworthy rather than inerrant.**

To speak more clearly, Boer suggests that the term infallible be defined by the terms reliable and trustworthy rather than by the term inerrant. Boer does not want to drop the term inerrant. He simply wants to limit its use to the abiding truths Jesus spoke and let the contradictory passages remain as a mystery about which no one has to worry his head.

The disparities posed by passages with differences, Boer says, can be solved only by artificial harmonizations or by various assumptions. Rather than "contriving an escape from embarrassment," he suggests an "excision" from the understanding of infallibility.[5] He suggests dropping "the conception that the

Bible as a human literary product is a book in which literary, historical, geographical, numerical, or other disparities do not and cannot exist." By this excision, Boer argues, the Christian is properly putting the infallibility of Scripture in its proper place as an article of faith that is to be believed but not proved, like other articles of faith such as creation, the deity of Christ, the atoning power of his death, his resurrection, the coming of the Holy Spirit, and others.

Such a view of infallibility, he says, will relieve the Christian mind of a great deal of tension. When discoveries are made that call into question certain data of Scripture, the Christian with a "true view of the infallibility of Scripture" will not be disturbed. The Christian does not surrender the Bible to the unbelieving critic to let him play fast and loose with it. He continues to see the whole of the Bible in terms of the adoring esteem of Psalm 119. "Standing on this rock that cannot be moved" the Christian can "afford fearless honesty in handling the human garment that both hides and reveals the infallibility with which the divine Author has spoken to us."[6] He then does not have to defend datings that cannot be defended, and he can acknowledge disparities when they are evident since he sees "a time-conditioned context as the bearer of a verity that cannot change."

Along this same line, Boer warns against setting up "standards for the reading and study of the Word of God that are not given or sanctioned by that Word."[7] He argues that the literal inerrancy of the Bible is a human deduction from the doctrine of inspiration. He concludes that the doctrine of literal inerrancy sets the scene "for an exegesis that is basically an exercise in the reading of the Bible in terms of the received tradition." This, he says, leads to the exclusion of any study of the Bible's relationship to the environment in which the writers grew up and through which they received their religious, cultural, and historical mindset.[8]

> **Inerrancy is a human deduction rather than something the Bible teaches.**

The mystery of creation

To avoid sterile exegesis Boer pleads that "Christians give full weight to the doctrine of creation and its implication for God's activity in history and nature."[9] God's redemptive activity did not take place in a vacuum but operated wholly within the context of creation. Thus there is an intertwining of the spiritual with the natural.

The world became imperfect after the Fall. But God did not cast off his creation. Instead he revived it, healed it, and made it serviceable again to his divine purpose.

Boer says that this same "linkage" exists between the work of the Redeemer God in things spiritual and the Creator God in things natural. This is evident in the Spirit's work of inspiring the sacred writings. Here, too, there is a constant intertwining of the spiritual with the natural and the historical. The "distinctly human element is everywhere in evidence in the composition of the sacred writings."[10] As a result there is "nothing that is obvious, self-evident, easily definable or analyzable about the primary work of the Holy Spirit."[11]

As God used an imperfect world to accomplish his purpose so the Holy Spirit uses an imperfect book to accomplish his purpose.

The Spirit, Boer says, works incognito. He hides his divinity in the garment of the human writers. God mysteriously used an imperfect creation after the Fall to accomplish his divine purpose. In the same way the Holy Spirit mysteriously uses a less than perfect book to accomplish his divine purpose. The Spirit allows the perfection of his work to be reflected in the "brokenness and imperfection" of the lives of the men who wrote the Bible.

The mystery of Scripture

Boer's conclusion is that, wherever the divine and the human meet, there is mystery. "It would not seem that the Holy Spirit's inspiration of Scripture is any more definable than is the relationship of the divine and the human in Christ."[12] Boer insists that those who accept the inability to define inspiration will also accept Jesus' words "Scripture cannot be broken" as a clear witness to the infallibility of Scripture. But they will define infallibility as the conformity of the written words to the truth, which only faith can discern.

The touchstone for Christians, Boer says, will not be the inerrancy of Scripture but an embracing of Jesus Christ in faith. Christians will not be indifferent to the clashing data and the contradictory phenomena in the Bible, but they will refuse to let the certainty of the unbreakable validity of the gospel be obscured by such things. They also will decline to attempt any contrived harmonizations, which somehow are supposed to strengthen faith by bringing disparities into the area of infallible revealed truth.

Analyzing Boer's approach

What is to be said about this approach? One thing that Boer stresses is valid, but much is not. His warning that Christians should not get so involved with the differences in Scripture that they lose sight of its essential message of salvation is well taken. But his understanding of Christology and of Scripture is seriously flawed.

What about the so-called problem passages of Scripture, particularly those in the synoptic gospels? The differences they present do not require "contrived harmonizations." Instead, if the following considerations are kept in mind, it becomes evident that though there are differences (properly defined), there are no contradictions (properly defined):

1. A distinction must be made between a difference (something that requires more than a passing glance to grasp fully) and a contradiction (something that is said to be both true and untrue about a given person in a certain place at a certain time).

2. Verbal inspiration does not always mean that the writers quoted verbatim every time they recorded what a person had said. Sometimes one writer quotes word for word and another summarizes the substance of what was said. This is a difference, but it is not a contradiction.

3. The order of recording does not always reflect the order in which things transpired. Matthew tends to give the accounts of miracles by grouping several together. Luke tends to tell about the miracles in the historical order in which they happened. This is a difference but not a contradiction.

4. The fact that one of the synoptic writers omits a detail does not mean he denies or is ignorant of that detail. When one writer omits a detail that another includes, this is a difference but not a contradiction.

5. Different emphases do not mean that the writers had different theologies.

6. For the sake of brevity a writer may simply present the substance of an event, as Matthew often does, while the details of the account are provided by another writer. This is a difference but not a contradiction.

7. Some of the differences are simply due to our lack of information. For instance, it was thought that some of Luke's historical references were in error. But the more we have learned about Roman history, the more this supposition has been proved to be incorrect.[13]

8. If we suggest a possible solution to a difference, it is not done as a prop for our faith. Rather, it helps show that the difference is due mainly to our lack of information. It also may be done to show that the unbeliever's conclusion that there must be a contradiction is not true.[14]

9. Jesus often repeated the same words and thoughts while teaching different audiences (sometimes crowds and sometimes disciples) at different times (such as in the Galilean ministry and the Perean ministry). Often these same words and thoughts took a slightly different form because of the different occasion. These really are not differences because the accounts are referring to different occasions, not giving an account of the same occasion.

10. The synoptic accounts are very similar because
   - The accounts are true.
   - The common outline is the life of Jesus.
   - Those who were eyewitnesses carefully followed the words of the apostles (Luke 1:2; 2 Peter 1:15).[15]

11. The accounts are different because
  - The writers had more material than they could possibly record.
  - Each was writing with a different purpose and selected material accordingly.
  - Each had a different writing style.

These are not strong-armed attempts to wrestle Scripture into a preconceived mold. These are simply the facts as they present themselves again and again when one studies each of the synoptics separately and then in harmony with one another.

Boer's Christology

What about Boer's Christology? Its basic error is that it fails to distinguish between the humanity of Christ and his humiliation. To put it another way, Boer mistakenly equates Christ's incarnation (his taking on a human nature) and his exinanition (his choosing not to make use of all his divine attributes at all times).

When Boer asserts that Jesus did not know everything because he was human, he errs. It was not because Jesus was human that he did not know everything. Rather, it was because in his state of humiliation (exinanition) he did not choose at all times to use fully the divine attribute of omniscience, which was communicated to his human nature in his incarnation.

Jesus knew all things (John 16:30) and at the same time he did not know all things (Mark 13:32). To us this is a psychological mystery. But his not knowing was not the result of his being a man. He is and always will be not only true God but also true man. In his state of exaltation he still possesses his human nature in personal union with his divine nature. To say, then, that Jesus did not know all things because he was a man would mean

The errors of Boer's Christology:

- Jesus did not know all things because he was human.
- The God-man accommodated himself to errors.

that also in his exaltation he does not know all things. No, it was part of his humiliation, not his incarnation, that Jesus did not fully use his omniscience at all times.

Furthermore, Jesus' exinanition does not mean, as Boer suggests, that he employed or even accommodated himself to "existing beliefs which were erroneous." Jesus was and is the truth (John 14:6), and without exception he bore witness to the truth (John 18:37). When Jesus spoke of Moses and Isaiah as the authors of the writings he quoted (John 5:46; Matthew 15:7), he was not just expressing himself, as Boer suggests, in terms of the "common deposit of belief" in those days about such matters. Jesus' human nature was never separated even for a moment from his divine nature. As the God-man he never deviated from that which is the absolute truth.

Boer's doctrine of Scripture

Boer puts an improper, unscriptural emphasis on the "human trappings" in which the divine Word is revealed. To say that "discrepancies" in Scripture compel us to view the Word of God as dressed in the literary garment of man, to say that inspiration does not protect the scriptural writings from being subject to human weaknesses, to say that the Bible is not only the Book among books but a book among books—none of these statements agree with what God says to his prophet: "I have put my words in your mouth" (Jeremiah 1:9), or to what Paul confesses: "We speak, not in words taught us by human wisdom but in words taught by the Spirit, expressing spiritual truths in spiritual words" (1 Corinthians 2:13).

Scripture does not explain the mystery of the process of inspiration. But when David declares, "The Spirit of the LORD spoke through me; his word was on my tongue" (2 Samuel 23:2), and when the psalmist describes his tongue as "the pen of a skillful writer" (Psalm 45:1), they are not asserting that the Spirit's divine work was hidden by the weakness and brokenness of their human words.

Inspiration was a unique process. The result was not an imperfect work that is an intertwining of the spiritual, which is absolute truth, and the natural and the historical, which are relative truth. The Bible is not an embodiment of the absolute truth of divine reality in the garb of the relative truth of the human record. Such descriptions of Scripture do not square with what happened according to 2 Timothy 3:16, "All Scripture is God-breathed," or 2 Peter 1:19-21, "We have the word of the prophets made more certain . . . No prophecy of Scripture came about by the prophet's own interpretation . . . but men spoke from God as they were carried along by the Holy Spirit."

> **Scripture is not a mixture of divine, absolute truth and human, relative truth.**

Boer's view implies that God does not assure us that everything in Scripture is infallible. He limits infallibility to those things in the area of divine certainty. Such a subjective limitation creates uncertainty as to whether a particular passage belongs to such certainty or not.

Boer undermines the doctrine of the inerrancy of Scripture further when he says that we dare not make Scripture what we want it to be rather than the way the writer's contemporaries were expected to read these writings. The warning is valid if it is aimed at a twisting of the Scriptures. But Boer implies instead that people back then spoke less exactly than what we expect today. There is no warrant, however, for the assumption that people of Jesus' time spoke any less exactly than we do today. Facts were facts then just as they are now, and people used rounded numerical figures and figures of speech in the same way and for the same purpose as people do today.

Boer's acceptance of the historical-critical method (oral, source, and redaction criticism) as a useful tool for Christians is based on the assumption that higher criticism is a technical exercise that is neutral in the hands of a true believer. The fact is, however, that the literary criticism of the historical-critical method is thoroughly rationalistic. This unbelieving approach cannot be divorced from the method itself because it is part and parcel of the unbelieving spirit with which the negative critic views how Scripture came into being.

Summary

The "conservative" position of Boer tries to say that the Scripture is infallible and yet it is not infallible, that it is inerrant and yet it is not inerrant, because it is a mysterious combination of both the divine and the human.

This approach is built on an erroneous view of both Christology and the doctrine of Scripture. The attempt to make the inspiration of the Bible a mystery of faith that allows the believer to be undisturbed by the "disparities" he meets in Scripture fails for the same reason the approaches of Bultmann and gospel reductionism do. It places man, at least in part, above Scripture as its analyst and critic. The subjectivity that this approach lets loose in the interpretation of Scripture can in time only wreak havoc with God's Word.

There are others like Boer. Some Lutherans and a growing number of conservative evangelicals attempt to uphold the basic idea of inerrancy while at the same time try to fit in with a "scholarly" view like Boer's of how the Bible came into being.[16] They declare that the historical-critical tools that are used to attack inerrancy are not totally destructive. If these rationalistic tools are used correctly, these men would like to have Christians believe, they may even be helpful in some ways. It is sad to see that those who want to uphold inerrancy do not realize that, by what may seem to be only a slight concession, they are really surrendering the position they so dearly wish to uphold.

NOTES

1. Harry H. Boer, *The Bible and Higher Criticism* (Grand Rapids: William B. Eerdmans Publishing Co., 1981).

2. *Ibid.,* p. 23.

3. *Ibid.,* p. 95.

4. *Ibid.,* p. 77.

5. *Ibid.,* p. 86.

6. *Ibid.*, p. 88.

7. *Ibid.*, p. 97.

8. *Ibid.*, pp. 100,101.

9. *Ibid.*, p. 101.

10. *Ibid.*, p. 104.

11. *Ibid.*, p. 106.

12. *Ibid.*, p. 109.

13. For example, for centuries some of Luke's historical statements were questioned (e.g., that there was a census when
Quirinius was governor, that the term *Judaea* in a broader
sense included Perea and Galilee, that Sergius Paulus
served in the office of proconsul on the island of Cyprus). As
more information has come to light on Roman history, one
by one, Luke's statements have been shown to be correct.

14. For example, in the account of the healing of blind Barti-
maeus, Matthew says it took place as Jesus went out of
Jericho while Mark and Luke say it took place on Jesus'
way into Jericho. For centuries this seemed to be a clear
contradiction because all three synoptic writers are referring to the same event. Archeological studies in the past
century, however, have revealed that at Jesus' time there
were two cities called Jericho, an old city going back in time
and a new city built closer to Jesus' time. It is possible that
Matthew, who writes for the Jews primarily, referred to the
old city, while Mark and Luke, who wrote for Gentiles primarily, referred to the new city. We need to be careful that
we do not make this "the solution" because further knowledge may suggest another solution to this seeming contradiction. The archeological solution does show, however, that
the unbelievers' conclusion that there must be a contradiction is not true.

15. Luke's words at the beginning of his gospel are often cited as
proof that all kinds of contradictory accounts of Jesus' life
were circulating at the time and that Luke wrote to set the
account of Jesus' life straight. A careful reading of Luke's
words reveals just the opposite. Note that Luke says that
the many accounts were drawn up "just as [the Greek means
'in exactly the same way as'] they were handed down" by the
apostles. So what was circulating was exactly what the apostles had told people about Jesus. And Luke adds that his

account would serve to assure Theophilus of "the certainty of the things" he had heard.

16. Several examples of this trend are:

   a. Robert Stein's theory stating that redaction criticism helps establish two "layers" of the divine Word: one layer being Jesus' original words, and the second layer being the evangelists' inspired interpretations of Jesus' original words. In the latter, he says, there may have been a little changing of what Jesus said or adding to what Jesus said (*The Synoptic Problem,* Grand Rapids: Baker Book House, 1987).

   b. D. A. Carson's, K. J. Vanhoozer's, Moises Silva's, and C. L. Blomberg's articles in *Hermeneutics, Authority and Canon* (Grand Rapids: Zondervan Publishing Corporation, 1986), which try to find something helpful in form, source, or redaction criticism while at the same time trying to uphold the "consistent truthfulness" of the Scriptures.

   c. Most of the books published by Zondervan, Baker, and Eerdmans in the late 1980s and 1990s listed under the bibliography for this chapter.

BIBLIOGRAPHY—CHAPTER TWELVE

Black, A. B., and D. S. Dockery. *New Testament Criticism and Interpretation.* Grand Rapids: Zondervan Publishing Corporation, 1991.

Boer, H. R. *The Bible and Higher Criticism.* Grand Rapids: William B. Eerdmans Publishing Co., 1978.

Bronson, M., and C. R. Padilla. *Conflict and Context—Hermeneutics in the Americas.* Grand Rapids: William B. Eerdmans Publishing Co., 1986.

Carson, D. A., and J. D Woodbridge (eds.). *Hermeneutics, Authority and Canon.* Grand Rapids: Zondervan Publishing Corporation, 1986.

_____ . *Scripture and Truth.* Grand Rapids: Baker Book House, 1992.

Conn, H. M. *Inerrancy and Hermeneutic: A Tradition, A Challenge, A Debate.* Grand Rapids: Baker Book House, 1988.

Erickson, M. J. *Evangelical Interpretation.* Grand Rapids: Zondervan Publishing Corporation, 1993.

Garrett, D. A., and R. R. Melick, Jr. *Authority and Interpretation.* Grand Rapids: Baker Book House, 1987.

Harrison, Waltke, Guthrie, and Fee. *Biblical Criticism: Historical, Literary and Textual.* Grand Rapids: Zondervan Publishing Corporation, 1978.

Inch, M. A., and C. H. Bullock (eds.). *The Literature and Meaning of Scripture.* Grand Rapids: Baker Book House, 1981.

Johnson, C. B. *The Psychology of Biblical Interpretation.* Grand Rapids: Zondervan Publishing Corporation, 1983.

Kaiser, W. C., and Moises Silva. *An Introduction to Biblical Hermeneutics.* Grand Rapids: Zondervan Publishing Corporation, 1994.

Linnemann, Eta. *Historical Criticism of the Bible, Methodology or Ideology.* Grand Rapids: Baker Book House, 1990.

_____. *Is There a Synoptic Problem?* Grand Rapids: Baker Book House, 1992.

Longman, T. *Literary Approaches to Biblical Interpretation.* Grand Rapids: Zondervan Publishing Corporation, 1987.

Marshall, I. H. *New Testament Interpretation.* Grand Rapids: William B. Eerdmans Publishing Co., 1977.

_____. *The Origins of New Testament Christology.* Downers Grove, IL: InterVarsity Press, 1976.

McKnight, S. *Interpreting the Synoptic Gospels.* Grand Rapids: Baker Book House, 1988.

_____. *Introducing New Testament Interpretation.* Grand Rapids: Baker Book House, 1990.

Rademacher, E., and R. Preus (eds.). *Hermeneutics, Inerrancy and the Bible.* Grand Rapids: Zondervan Publishing Corporation, 1984.

Silva, Moises. *Has the Church Misread the Bible?* Grand Rapids: Zondervan Publishing Corporation, 1987.

13

A COMPARATIVE EVALUATION
OF THESE THREE APPROACHES
OF THE HISTORICAL-CRITICAL METHOD

Six touchstones

The three previous chapters have presented three forms of the historical-critical method of interpretation. One is characterized by existential demythologizing, the second by gospel reductionism, and the third by a divine-human mystery approach. All three accept the literary criticism of rationalism (oral, source, and redaction criticism) as useful. As a result, these three approaches have more in common with one another than they have with the true scriptural method of interpretation.

The truth of this assertion can be demonstrated by examining all three approaches by six touchstones. What each approach really says about Scripture is revealed by noting what each says about the clarity of Scripture, Scripture as history, Scripture as revelation, the unity of Scripture, the authority of Scripture, and Scripture's message of salvation.

Is Scripture:

- **clear?**
- **history?**
- **revelation?**
- **unified?**
- **authoritative?**
- **the message of salvation?**

This kind of examination is important because the proponent of a faulty approach often hides limitations that he places on any one of these six items. However, he can't do this if he is asked to declare not only what he believes about them but also what he does not believe about them.

When this is done with these three approaches of the historical-critical method, it readily becomes apparent (as this chapter will show) that the differences between the three are not a matter of substance but one of degree. To say it another way, it is not a matter of good or bad—but of bad, worse, and worst.

The clarity of Scripture

Is Scripture clear in what it says and means? In following any one of these three approaches, it is obvious from the outset that no one but the "scholar" is prepared to apply the intricacies of rationalistic literary criticism: form criticism, source criticism, redaction criticism, and comparative religious study. So, everyone is really dependent on the "scholar" to clarify much of what the New Testament says to him.

When we see that the "scholars" often disagree in their conclusions, it is obvious that Scripture isn't very clear for the "scholar" either. In short, for anyone who uses rationalistic literary criticism, the clarity of Scripture has become a subjective matter.

In **existential demythologizing** the subjectivity results from the fact that demythologizing is really the old allegorizing of the Middle Ages in new dress. But this modern type of allegory is even more subjective because there is no body of doctrine, such as the tradition of the church was in the Middle Ages, as a point of reference for the interpreter. The goal of finding one's "true existence" or "authentic being" is the only restraint on the subjectivity of the interpreter.

Gospel reductionism restricts the clarity of Scripture to those places where the gospel is taught. But casting doubt on the rest of Scripture has in turn led to a loss of clarity as to what the gospel is. Clear statements of Scripture are no longer regarded as clear. Rather, each person is encouraged to find what Scripture means to him. However, he is warned not to try to impose on others what he understands Scripture to be saying, not even in regard to the gospel. This, too, is not clarity but subjectivity.

In the first two approaches this subjectivity is not considered a weakness. Instead, it is applauded because it supposedly rids the church of a fixed meaning for any Bible passage ("dogmatism") and leaves the meaning of the text open. Any danger posed by having an open text can be overcome, it is said, by the sharing of insights. In this way the subjectivity of one person will be tempered by the insights of others if anyone tends to drift too far from the mainstream.

SCRIPTURE is an "open text."

The **divine-human mystery approach** tries to temper subjectivity by setting aside any passages that contain "disparities." They are not to be discussed. But who serves as the final judge to decide whether or not a passage contains a disparity? One person may stop with a few "difficulties" in the synoptics. Another person may see many other passages as being part of the human garment in which the Word of God is dressed.

In all three approaches which employ the historical-critical method, the clarity of Scripture is compromised by some kind of subjectivity. Scripture is not considered clear in all that it says and means. The individual is free to find his own meaning or to omit a verse or a number of verses from discussion.

Scripture as history

In subjecting the historical portions of Scripture to rationalistic literary criticism, the supernatural is either denied or questioned or limited. **Existential demythologizing** denies the supernatural. **Gospel reductionism** allows the possibility of the supernatural but questions its probability. The

divine-human mystery approach limits the supernatural by its being intertwined with human disparities.

In all three approaches, therefore, the human characteristic of the history contained in the New Testament is given undue emphasis in some way. For **existential demythologizing,** this means that very little is known about Jesus. Kaesemann writes in *Essays on New Testament Themes:*

> We know nothing at all about the latter (i.e., Jesus' exterior) save only the way which led from Galilee to Jerusalem, from the preaching of the God (who is near us) to the hatred of official Judaism and execution by the Romans. Only an uncontrolled imagination could have the self-confidence to weave out of these pitiful threads the fabric of history in which cause and effect could be determined in detail. But conversely . . . we need not let defeatism and skepticism have the last word. . . . The primitive Christian community did identify the exalted Lord with the earthly Jesus . . . [There are] still a few pieces of the Synoptic tradition which the historian has to acknowledge as authentic.[1]

For the **gospel reductionist** the fact that the history of the New Testament is the reporting of the church means that the interpreter is free to decide what he thinks was meant to be historical. In this way the kerygma is not necessarily denied or accepted as history, but the emphasis is shifted almost entirely to the spiritual message of the kerygma.

> Any approach to the Scriptures which focuses on the need for historical factuality rather than on the primary need for Christ leads us away from Christ rather than to him. . . . The fact that a given biblical episode is historical is not important in and of itself. The importance of such historical events lies in what God was doing in and through them. . . . Even though we may not be able to harmonize discrepancies which appear in the New Testament Gospel accounts, that fact does not shake our faith or invalidate these accounts as Word of God. Our faith rests in the promise of a faithful God, not in the accuracy of ancient historians.[2]

The difference between the first two approaches, then, is more of a difference in degree than in kind. The clear testimony of Scripture that a given text is historical will be denied by one and ignored by the other. Both maintain that truth exists in the Bible, but they insist that the Bible conveys this truth, not through the statement of historical facts, but in the form of historical narrative. The parables of Jesus, especially a parable like the one about the good Samaritan, will be cited as examples

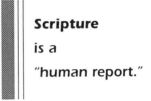

Scripture is a "human report."

of how a spiritual message can be taught without the necessity of knowing whether an event really happened or not.

In these two approaches the miraculous events by which God in his grace completed our salvation are allegorized or "spiritualized." In place of historical events that are central to the Christian faith, "scholars" offer a God who supposedly saves man by his words or his Promise. God's actions recorded as history in the Bible are either explained away or put into the background.

In the **divine-human mystery approach** the historical nature of events is still emphasized, but the accuracy of the historical record is limited by what is called the incarnation of the Bible. The claim is made that faith can overleap any historical inaccuracies caused by the human garment, which hides divine realities from those who do not have faith. Perhaps unwittingly, yet undeniably, this subjection of the history in Scripture to the scalpel of human judgment opens the door for eventual major surgery.

The Bible as revelation

Some historical-critical interpreters may object to being classified as belonging to a group that denies revelation. Again, there is a difference in degree. The first two approaches both deny divine revelation as information from God mediated through chosen writers in simple intelligible words and concepts at a time in the distant past. Instead, revelation is a modern event.

In **existential demythologizing** the New Testament text is not objec-

REVELATION is a "modern event."

tive revelation but a "witness to the drama of God's dialogue with man in connection with Christ." As a person hears this "witness," it becomes the means by which God's presence in judgment and promise dawns on him with the same freshness and excitement as it did in Christ.

Revelation, then, is not the words recorded in the Bible but the experience the individual has when he becomes aware that these words are the story of his own life, the story of how God wants to fashion him to be his authentic self. Kaesemann writes in *Essays on New Testament Themes:*

> Revelation ceases to be God's revelation once it has been brought within a causal nexus. . . . It does not convey to me an idea or program; it is an act which lays hold on me.[3]

Gospel reductionism does not deny that the gospel content of the Bible may have been a revelation to the early Christian church. However, this gospel is mingled with the kerygma of the early church with its interpretations and historical inaccuracies. So the important thing is not what God revealed to them then but what he reveals to the reader by those words today.

Making revelation a modern event cuts it loose from the objective meaning of the words. It allows the modern reader a great deal of subjectivity in his personal "encounter" with God in the words of Scripture or in the Promise contained in these words. The disastrous results of such a view of revelation will become more obvious in the last three touchstones.

The **divine-human mystery approach** does insist that the Bible is a revelation by God to the early church. Yet by drawing a distinction between the exactness with which God spoke then and how we speak in our modern day, revelation is also cut loose in part from the objective meaning of the words. This in turn allows the modern reader some subjectivity in dealing with these words. The suggestion is made that a person should just ignore the disparities caused by the difference between how speaking in exact terms was viewed then and how it is viewed now. This suggestion must be rejected because this difference is not real. It is simply one of the lies Satan uses to introduce the yeast of subjectivity into the matter of revelation in order for it to do its disastrous work.

The unity of Scripture

The adherents of **existential demythologizing** declare that saying the Bible is a perfect unity is a sure sign of theological immaturity. They maintain that the following points are obvious to any honest Bible reader:

- The Old Testament reflects a tribal religion while the New Testament reflects a religious philosophy.
- There is a conflict between Jesus' statements on love and his eschatological pronouncements.
- Jesus and Paul differ with one another because the former preaches love and the latter atonement.
- James and Hebrews do not agree with Paul on justification.
- John's understanding of faith is unique.
- The New Testament either reinterprets or rejects the Old Testament law.
- There are endless historical discrepancies.

The listing could go on. Just as a person who has a problem but refuses to admit it has failed to take the first step in solving his problem, so it is said that any view of an underlying unity of the Bible only hinders any real progress in solving the "problems" of interpreting the Bible.

Gospel reductionism insists that there is at least one unity in Scripture, namely in God's proclamation of the message of judgment and mercy. However, when one asks what this message is, it becomes obvious that the disunity among those who follow this approach allows only the vaguest of definitions of this message. It is clear, therefore, that unity in regard to the gospel is also lacking. Could anything else be expected of a method of interpretation that makes

> **To say that the Bible has a "perfect unity" is a sure sign of "theological immaturity."**

the clarity of Scripture subjective, the historicity of Scripture questionable, and the revelation of Scripture a modern event?

The **divine-human mystery approach** insists that to say that the Scriptures form a perfect harmony without contradictory phenomena and inconsistencies is a failure to take the human quality of Scripture seriously. This, too, is placing the unity of Scripture into the subjective hands of the Bible critic.

All three approaches of the historical-critical method allow the question as to whether or not there is unity in Scripture to become a matter of individual judgment, at least in part. In this way all three also undermine the basic unity of the Bible.

The authority of Scripture

Since the clarity, historicity, revelation, and unity of Scripture are undermined in some way, it is not surprising that the authority of Scripture will suffer also. If all the foregoing are a matter of subjective determination at least in part, how could anyone say that the Bible is authoritative without being challenged?

To say that the Bible is the sole and final authority is "bibliolatry."

In fact, some of the proponents of the historical-critical method say that anyone who makes the Bible the sole and final norm for the church fails to remember that God, not a book, is Lord of the church. To make Scripture authoritative is labeled "bibliolatry."

Such an antithesis that sets the authority of God against the authority of the Bible ignores the simple fact that God himself has made his Word authoritative for us. Those who deny this fact will trumpet the need to remain free from doctrinal statements even though they are based on Scripture. Doctrinal statements of any kind, they argue, legalistically impose control of thought and action on a liberated child of God.

In **existential demythologizing,** since the Bible supposedly becomes God's Word only in the kerygmatic encounter, the authority of Scripture is only that which is experienced by the individual in his own personal decision of response. In

gospel reductionism the Bible's authority is defined as its power to accomplish its purpose of saving mankind. The Bible, it is said, is not a source book of doctrine or the norm of faith. The Bible is not an authority that determines what is to be believed. It is our authority for daring to trust that God has kindly intentions toward us. In short, the Bible is not an authority in what it says to us but in what it does for us.

In the first two approaches, then, the Scripture has no objective authority. Instead, the Bible as the norm is replaced by dozens of "scholars" saying "the norm for me is . . ." In most seminaries, and eventually in most pulpits, a doctrinal smorgasbord of the writings of various "scholars" is served, and the individual student or layperson is urged to select the norm that best suits his existential situation or his gospel understanding.

In the **divine-human mystery approach,** the authority of Scripture is supposedly upheld. Yet this is done by setting aside some historical passages that reveal themselves as the human garb in which the absolute truths are clothed. This, too, is a limiting of the authority of Scripture. To assert that these "human qualities" of Scripture have nothing to do with the essence of Scripture is simply Satan's way of getting his foot in the door in order to spread his attack on the authority of the rest of the Bible.

Scripture's message of salvation

The most tragic result of the historical-critical method is what it does to the message of salvation.

For those who follow **existential demythologizing,** salvation is equated with authentic existence. In this view, the individual sets himself free as Christ did by accepting the challenge of God's Word to rid himself of all materialistic anxieties and to open himself to God to live in love.

Existential salvation is supposed to be a modern route between the outdated idea of sin and grace and the bankrupt skepticism of 19th-

SALVATION is finding one's "authentic existence."

century rationalism. But the devilish character of existential demythologizing can be seen from these three characteristics:

1. Its philosophical nature presents a strong appeal to the human intellect. Salvation is not God's work in Christ, which is simply accepted by faith, but it is a matter of the human mind searching for true existence.

2. In turn, its definition of true existence challenges man to rid himself of his materialistic and selfish desire for "things" and challenges him instead to adopt an unselfish life of service to his fellowmen. This challenge satisfies the large number of people who feel that the main purpose religion serves is to promote love among mankind.

3. At the same time, its use of all the basic biblical terms deceives many into thinking that it is truly Christian. The pastor still teaches that "salvation" is by "God's grace" through "faith" in "Christ" and that this "truth" is based on what the "whole Bible" says.

What about the 18 centuries of Christianity that did not understand these biblical terms as they are used in existential demythologizing? One is told that he ought not concern himself with the past but only with the present. That is what existentialism is all about.

Or, one is told that in its basic form the Bible served the people of ancient and medieval times well because it conformed with their supernatural worldview. If some people today still have this outdated view, the Bible will help them find their true existence in the traditional meaning of the terms *sin* and *grace*. However, for those who have the modern, scientific worldview, a new approach to the Bible is needed. This is necessary if the Bible is to fulfill its purpose of helping modern man find his true being.

The "miracle" of the biblical language, it is said, is that it enables Scripture to serve well in two totally different worldviews.

In **gospel reductionism,** the narrowing of the divine side of God's Word to its gospel content also undermines the clarity, unity, historicity, and authority of much of Scripture. This leaven in turn also affects a clear understanding of the gospel.

No single, simple definition of the gospel is acceptable to all. Instead, some vague definitions of the gospel are given. It is said that, since the Bible presents a rich variety of ways to portray the word of Promise, one ought not try to impose on another his own particular way of wording the gospel. It is enough to agree that God's promise begets and preserves in the believer's heart a confidence that God was and is at work in human history to bring blessings to the human family. Note how the

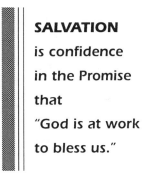

SALVATION is confidence in the Promise that "God is at work to bless us."

definition of the gospel has been made so broad that anyone can put his own meaning into it.

It may be true that not all who embrace gospel reductionism have lost an understanding of the true gospel. But those who have not lost it yet are in grave danger of doing so. The attempt to maintain the gospel while denying the importance and factuality of the historical events on which the gospel is founded is an impossible task. One does not have to be a prophet to foretell this. All one has to do is apply the scriptural truth that a little yeast introduced into some dough will eventually work through the whole batch.

In general, those who follow an approach similar to the **divine-human mystery approach** still hold the understanding that salvation is by faith in Christ's redeeming work. But the introduction of an erroneous Christology to undergird an erroneous doctrine of Scripture is a deadly combination of yeast that will do its devastating work if it is not quickly removed.

Summary

A capsule chart of what all three approaches say about the six points discussed in this chapter may be helpful. Note that the limiting word "only" appears in every answer. This one word reveals clearly that these three approaches have more in common with one another than they do with a truly scriptural view. It is these limitations that can easily be hidden by the adherents of the historical-critical method if their answers to each question are not closely examined.

Key: ED =   existential demythologizing
      GR =   gospel reductionism
      DHM =   divine-human mystery

Is the Bible clear?

ED: The Bible is clear <u>only</u> in what it means, not in what it says.
GR: The Bible is clear <u>only</u> in what the gospel promises.
DHM: The Bible is clear <u>only</u> where it does not contain disparities.

Is the Bible history?

ED: The Bible is history <u>only</u> as a record of the writer's subjective view of events, not as a record of historical facts.
GR: The Bible is history <u>only</u> in those portions that one determines the writer meant to be historical fact and not his own view of events.
DHM: The Bible is history <u>only</u> when what is written is not colored by the human environment in which the writer received his mindset.

Is the Bible revelation?

ED: <u>Only</u> as a modern event in the kerygmatic encounter, not as doctrine.
GR: <u>Only</u> as a modern event in addressing the Promise to man, not as doctrine.
DHM: <u>Only</u> when God speaks through the human writers with the same kind of exactness with which we are familiar in our modern times.

Is the Bible a perfect unit?

ED: <u>Only</u> insofar as the 'exalted Christ' of the kerygma has some ties by a few thin threads to the historical Jesus.
GR: <u>Only</u> in those passages that contain law and gospel.
DHM: <u>Only</u> when the contradictions that are part of the human garment of Scripture are set aside.

Is the Bible authoritative?

ED: <u>Only</u> for each individual in his personal "Christ event."
GR: <u>Only</u> in its ability to bring people to trust the Promise.
DHM: <u>Only</u> in the divine certitude that is the unbreakable validity of the gospel.

Does the Bible teach salvation by grace through faith?

ED: <u>Only</u> in the sense of "authentic existence."
GR: <u>Only</u> in the way each individual understands God's word of promise.
DHM: <u>Only</u> as a book that reveals human weaknesses that are intertwined with this divine verity.

NOTES

1. Ernst Kaesemann, *Essays on New Testament Themes* (Naperville, IL: Allenson, 1964), p. 45.
2. Herman Otten, ed., "Faithful to Our Calling—Faithful to Our Lord," *A Christian Handbook on Vital Issues* (New Haven, MO: Leader Publishing Co., Inc., 1973), p. 824.
3. Ernst Kaesemann, *op. cit.*, p. 31.

BIBLIOGRAPHY—CHAPTER THIRTEEN

McKim, D. K. *A Guide to Contemporary Hermeneutics.* Grand Rapids: William B. Eerdmans Publishing Co., 1986.

Woodbridge, J. D. *Biblical Authority.* Grand Rapids: Zondervan Publishing Corporation, 1982.

Marquardt, K. "The Incompatibility Between Historical-Critical Theology and the Lutheran Confessions." *Studies in Lutheran Hermeneutics.* Philadelphia: Fortress Press, 1978.

A Comparative Study of Varying Contemporary Approaches to Biblical Interpretation (A pamphlet published by the Commission on Theology and Church Relations of the Lutheran Church—Missouri Synod in March, 1973).

POSTSCRIPT

"GUARD THE GOOD DEPOSIT"

"It's just a matter of interpretation." In the Introduction it was noted that this lie of the devil is often cited to give credence to the idea that the words of the Bible can be interpreted in many different ways. The goal of this book was to show that the proper interpretation of God's inspired Word is never a matter of subjective opinion.

Part Two of this book showed how down through the years Satan has tried in different ways to undermine the proper interpretation of God's Word. Part Three showed that the historical-critical method has become the prevailing way of interpreting the Bible in most of the churches of our day—Catholic, Protestant, and Lutheran. Never before in the history of the church has Satan undermined both God's Word and the saving truth it teaches as quickly and as thoroughly in the hearts of so many Christians as he has with this method of interpretation.

We need to be on our guard against every sly approach that Satan uses to attack the truth of God's Word in our day. Peter warns us to be alert because our enemy the devil prowls around like a roaring lion looking for someone to devour (1 Peter 5:8). Paul tells us that the devil's methods will not always be out in the open because Satan will masquerade as an angel of light and his servants will masquerade as servants of righteousness (2 Corinthians 11:14,15).

Paul urged Timothy: "Guard the good deposit that was entrusted to you—guard it with the help of the Holy Spirit who lives in us" (2 Timothy 1:14). These words apply to us in our day also because the advent of the historical-critical method shows us that Satan is no less dangerous than he ever was.

In order to "guard the good deposit," each of our called pastors and teachers must be an interpreter who can be described "as one approved, a workman who does not need to be ashamed and who correctly handles the word of truth" (2 Timothy 2:15). It is equally important that every layperson understands the principles of proper interpretation and uses them in reading the Bible.

The only way that the "good deposit" handed down to us by the inspired writers can be maintained is if we use the method of interpretation restored to us by God's servant Luther. Let Scripture interpret Scripture. This is the only way we can avoid having any of the subjective ideas of men mixed with God's pure Word. This is the only way that God alone tells us both what the words of Scripture say and what they mean.

Guarding the good deposit in our day includes this that all of us know and use the principles of interpretation explained in Part One. As we use these principles and let Scripture interpret Scripture, the Holy Spirit will guard us from Satan's lies and guide us in the proper understanding of what God's Word means and says. May God always help us use these principles to this end!